Galatians

GALATIANS

John Fenton

The Bible Reading Fellowship
OPENING THE BIBLE

Published by
The Bible Reading Fellowship
Peter's Way, Sandy Lane West
Oxford OX4 5HG
ISBN 0 7459 3281 9
Albatross Books Pty Ltd
PO Box 320, Sutherland
NSW 2232, Australia
ISBN 0 7324 1556 X

First edition 1996
10 9 8 7 6 5 4 3 2 1 0

Acknowledgments
Unless otherwise stated, scripture quotations
are taken from the New Revised Standard
Version of the Bible copyright © 1989 by the
Division of Christian Education of the
National Council of the Churches of Christ in
USA.

A catalogue record for this book is
available from the British Library.

Printed and bound in Great Britain
by Cox and Wyman Limited, Reading

Contents

Introduction

Some time in the middle first century AD this letter from Paul was brought by a messenger to be read to the Christian communities that Paul had established in Asia Minor (modern Turkey).

We know enough from the letter itself and from other early Christian writings to understand much of what Paul is saying. But there are some questions to which we do not know the answer. We do not know for certain where Paul was when he wrote to the Galatians, or where exactly they lived. Nor do we know how many churches there were, to which he sent the letter.

We can work out to some extent how the situation that provoked it had come about, although there is still much uncertainty about this. But we can understand enough of what Paul is saying in the letter to realize that it was, and still is, a document of the greatest importance.

The letter will have been read out in full, from beginning to end, in each community. This would not have taken long—probably less than one hour. You would find it a useful preliminary to the study of this book on Galatians to put yourself in the same position as its first recipients by reading the letter straight through from beginning to end at one sitting. It does not matter which translation you use, but the one quoted in this book is *New Revised Standard Version* 1989 (NRSV). The abbreviation REB refers to the Revised English Bible (1989). As you read, remember that the divisions into chapters and verses which we are so familiar with in our printed Bibles were not invented until many centuries later.

There will of course be a vast difference between what the first recipients of the letter heard, and what we shall hear. They knew what the situation was that moved Paul to write to them—but we do not. Not until we have pieced together (from what Paul says in this letter and his other letters) what it was that had happened.

One thing will become clear immediately Paul's words are read. There was a row going on, and Paul is angry with some of those to whom he is writing. He addresses them as 'you foolish Galatians!' (3:1). There are some whom he does not name but against whom he utters threats: 'Let that one be accursed!' (1:8–9). Somebody has been saying things in Galatia and Paul is amazed that his converts have listened to them and begun to practise what was preached.

The row is about how one should live as a Christian; and that depends on what one believes about God and about what he requires of Christian people.

This may seem surprising, because the events we are concerned with happened within less than thirty years of the crucifixion and resurrection of Jesus in Jerusalem (which was probably in about AD30).

Some of the original followers of Jesus were still alive and Paul had met them. He refers to them in this letter as people about whom the Galatians will not need any further explanation and calls them simply 'James and Cephas [i.e. Peter] and John' (2:9).

We might think that at a time so close to its founder the church must have been united in faith and love. This letter shows that it was not so. There have been conflicts and disagreements in the history of Christianity from as far back as we can go.

It is not surprising that Jesus is quoted by Matthew as saying, 'Do not think that I have come to bring peace to the earth; I have not come to bring peace, but a sword' (10:34). This sword divided the followers of Jesus from those who did not believe in him and also divided the followers themselves into rival groups. The letter to the Galatians is firsthand evidence for the absence of peace from among Christians in the middle of the first century.

The Galatians themselves, of course, knew who their troublemakers were and what they had said. We can be fairly sure what it was they said but less certain who they were.

The main point of their message to the Galatians concerned what we call the Old Testament. But in those days those writings would have been referred to as 'the scriptures' or 'the scripture' (3:8, 22 and 4:30) or 'the law' (4:21). At the time when Galatians was written, the 'scriptures' involved in the dispute were the sacred books of the Jews, available to Greek-speaking readers in a translation known as the Septuagint. Neither the four Gospels nor any other Christian writings that we have now were in existence then, except possibly some earlier letters of Paul (e.g. 1 Thessalonians).

The opponents of Paul were saying that all Christians, whether they had been Jews before they were converted or Gentiles, should accept the scriptures in the same way—as books that contained authoritative rules for believers without any adjustments or modifications.

If this view had been accepted it would have had far-reaching results. People who had not been brought up as Jews (but who through Paul's preaching had believed in God and Jesus and been baptized) would have had to become members of Israel by circumcision (if they were males) and to have kept the whole of the Law of Moses as set out in the first five books of the Bible. They would have had to refrain from eating food that was classed as unclean. They would have had to adjust their lives so that they did no work from Friday evening till Saturday evening in order that they might keep the sabbath every week. And there would have been a lot of other things as well.

We might think that such a message delivered to non-Jewish people would not have been popular. But we would be wrong. The evidence shows that the Galatians were thrilled with the idea of adopting these ancient customs. They were, they believed, sanctified by continuous practice that went back to the time of Moses and the exodus of the Israelites from Egypt—and even earlier than that, to Abraham and the patriarchs, as described in the early chapters of Genesis.

It is sometimes said that the first century AD was an age of anxiety in which many people felt rootless and insecure. But if you accepted the Law of Moses that would establish you as a member of an ancient people. You would have roots, and you could call Abraham your father and Sarah your mother. You would have an unrivalled genealogy and status, and you would belong to an institution that was more ancient than any competitor. You would be inside a privileged circle and no longer an outsider.

Paul says to the Galatians that 'You are observing special days, and months, and seasons, and years' (4:10)—which meant that they were observing the calendar of Jewish feasts and festivals. And they were not finding it a burden. Just the opposite. It was a delight and a benefit. A set of procedures that made them feel safe in a fast-changing world. If it had not been so Paul would have had no need to write to the Galatians to tell them to stop it. Nor would he have been so angry with those who were promoting these ideas among the Galatian churches.

To first-century people who had not been brought up as Jews the idea of keeping the Law of Moses was very attractive—and so were the arguments that could be employed to persuade them to adopt this way of life. Our appreciation of Paul's letter will be greatly deepened if we can see what powerful and apparently irresistible arguments his opponents could call into service.

If we had we been living in Galatia at the time we might have been won over by Paul's opponents. We are immensely dependent on the benefit of hindsight. We know who won in the long run and what had happened to Christianity by the middle of the second century. Paul and his contemporaries did not. They could only weigh up arguments as they saw them at the time and to many people the arguments against Paul must have seemed irrefutable. They were straightforward and appealed to common sense whereas Paul's case must have appeared involved and unrealistic.

The opponents of Paul could say first of all that scripture was on their side. If the problem were raised in the form 'What must we do to belong to the people of God?', then the answer according to scripture was absolutely clear. God had told Abraham: 'Any uncircumcised male who is not circumcised in the flesh of his foreskin shall be cut off from his people; he has broken my covenant' (Genesis 17:14).

Both sides in the Galatian controversy appealed to scripture as the authority for what they were saying. But it cannot be denied that the opponents of Paul had the better claim to be doing what was clearly and unequivocally commanded in the Law.

These same opponents could have pointed out, secondly, that Jesus (and all the first disciples who had followed him in Galilee and Judea) had been circumcised. The circumcision of Jesus is recorded in only one of the four Gospels (Luke 2:21). But although that Gospel had not been written at the time of the controversy it would have been impossible to suppose that Mary and Joseph would not have seen to this on the eighth day after his birth, as the Law required. So if the founder of the movement and the foundation members had all kept the Law how could some later followers not do the same?

Thirdly, if one had asked at that time where authority was to be found and which church was the model for all other churches there was only one possible answer: the church in Jerusalem. The eleven disciples had moved there from Galilee after the resurrection—perhaps because of the expectation that the Lord would come from heaven to Jerusalem for the last judgment, and therefore they would be nearer to the place where he would arrive: 'On that day his feet shall stand on the Mount of Olives, which lies before Jerusalem on the east' (Zechariah 14:4).

James the Lord's brother became the leader of the Jerusalem church (he is mentioned in Galatians 1:19; 2:9, 12), and they would all have been circumcised and observant Jews. By what sort of reasoning could one avoid the conclusion that what was right in Jerusalem was not right elsewhere? Theology and church practice could not be subject to geography. If the church at the centre kept the Law of Moses, so should the churches on the circumference. Gentile sinners, as Paul calls them (2:15), were the last people to say what was right and what was wrong.

Fourthly, although Galilee and Judea had large non-Jewish populations at the time of Jesus, there is very little evidence that he had had dealings with Gentiles. There had been the Syrophoenician woman (Mark 7:24–30) and the centurion (Matthew 8:5–13; Luke 7:1–10). But in both cases their non-Jewish status had been noted as exceptional and the cures had been performed at a distance. Jesus had not entered their houses. Moreover there were traditions that Jesus had sent the twelve disciples to Israel only, not to Samaritans and not to Gentiles (Matthew 10:5f.).

We can imagine arguments along the lines: 'If the Lord did not deal with Gentiles while he was with us in the flesh how can we possibly go against his practice now? Surely Gentiles must become Jews in order to be members of the people of God? We have the authority of the Lord's usual practice for this, and nothing he said ever contradicted it.'

This is the attitude of Peter as it is described in Acts 10 and 11. He and others regard association with Gentiles, and eating unclean food, as a new revelation from God—not as something the Lord had commanded before his death and resurrection.

Those who troubled the Gentiles had still more arguments had they needed them, which must have seemed persuasive to Paul's converts. All over the area where they lived there would have been synagogues attended by local Jewish residents on Saturdays. Paul preached in them and built on traditions that the synagogues preserved. He expects his readers in Galatia to know about Abraham, Moses and the prophets. Though a Gentile could have associate-member status in the synagogue (i.e. be a God-fearer), one could not be a full member without keeping the commandments, particularly circumcision, the sabbath and the dietary laws.

The Jews would never have thought that these commandments would be changed or rescinded. They had fought a war in the second century BC (the Maccabean revolt) in order to maintain their right to do these things and they had won. Their ancestors had died fighting for this freedom and books about them were still being written in the first century AD. To say that these laws were now out of date was as much as to say that the martyrs had died to no purpose.

Or we can imagine an argument of this kind: 'Jesus commanded us to love. But how can we love the other members of the people of God without adopting their ways? Paul does this himself,' the argument would have gone on, 'and he admits it: When he is with Jews he lives as a Jew (1 Corinthians 9:20). We live with Jews here in Galatia. So shouldn't we live as Jews and accept their terms for admission to their community?'

Finally, we need to recall that no Christian in those days expected that history would still be continuing nearly two thousand years later. Both Paul and his opponents would have expected the Lord to return in their lifetime. 'We will not all die, but we will all be changed, in a moment, in the twinkling of an eye, at the last trumpet' (1 Corinthians 15:51–52). They were praying for the Lord to come and to come quickly. So it would seem odd to suppose that there should be separate and parallel arrangements for Christians who had been Jews and those who had been Gentiles.

There were, they thought, only a few years to run. Charity and convenience would both urge them in favour of a common lifestyle. It was the lifestyle of the patriarchs, the people of God in the past, and of Jesus and his apostles. It was also the lifestyle of the church in Jerusalem and those who had brought the 'full-gospel' to Galatia in order to correct the errors of Paul—someone who had never known the Lord 'in the flesh' and who was a one-time persecutor of the faith.

Paul faced a barrage of excellent, knock-down arguments and it must have seemed as if his opponents had all the trumps. If we had been Galatians we would certainly have been impressed by their persuasiveness. What can Paul say to win us over to his side?

His method is selective. He never quotes Genesis 17:12–14, the passage that is so explicit on the permanence of the law concerning circumcision ('throughout your generations'). He quotes other parts of Genesis—from chapters 15, 16, 17, and 18—but not the passage concerning circumcision. If we had asked him how to explain this commandment he would probably have said that it was an ordinance that was intended to apply only until Christ came. Similarly, he never quotes words of Jesus explicitly in this letter. He never uses an argument in the form: 'The Lord said this, therefore we must do it.' He quotes scripture frequently, probably because his opponents were doing so and he had to do the same when he answered them. But his authority for saying what he believes is not based on scripture as theirs may have been. He interprets scripture in the light of a faith that depends on something else—and he uses the passages from the Old Testament to illustrate this faith.

He explains this in a letter to the Corinthians: 'Whenever Moses is read [to those who do not believe], a veil lies over their minds; but when one turns to the Lord, the veil is removed (2 Corinthians 3:15–16). Faith comes first and the interpretation of scripture depends on that.

What is the ground of Paul's faith? As we read this letter we notice again and again that Paul refers to a series of events that have taken place in the recent past—mainly in the previous twenty years or so. The birth of Jesus and his death and resurrection are the beginning of the series. The conversion of Paul from being a zealous observer of the Law and persecutor of the church to being a preacher, comes next. His relations with the church in Jerusalem is also part of the series, and a particular incident when Peter was with Paul in Antioch.

Then there is Paul's first visit to the Galatians and the result of it— their faith in the Gospel and what the Spirit did to them: 'Did you experience so much for nothing?' he asks them (3:4). Almost the last words of the letter draw attention once more to what has certainly happened. If they look at Paul's body they will see the marks left by the beatings he had received in the synagogues (6:17). These marks show that he preaches a message that angers those who keep the Law: 'Why am I still being persecuted if I am still preaching circumcision? In that case the offence of the cross has been removed' (5:11).

'Getting into a rut' is a common experience. We can see only a certain set of facts—and they all seem to point one way and to require only one conclusion. The person who can help those who are in this state is the one who can show that there are more facts to be taken into account; and that when this is done they point to a very different conclusion.

This is what Paul is doing, in his letter to the Galatians. He uses recent events that have occurred in the lifetime of many of his readers—the death and resurrection of Jesus, his own conversion from Judaism to Christianity, his encounter with the leaders of the Jerusalem church and with the synagogues, and the origin and subsequent history of the churches in Galatia—to show that God is dealing with human beings in a different way now from what he had done in the past.

The result of this is that believers have a freedom that nobody had ever known before. If they would reflect on what had happened to them they would see that they had been brought into a new relationship with God and with one another that they had not enjoyed previously. It would be foolish to return to the state they were in before Paul had preached the gospel to them.

The permanent value of Paul's letter to the Galatians is that it reminds those who read it of the advantages they have as believers. The crucial point is not that they have come to know God but that God has come to know them (4:9).

The good news is always more than we can adequately retain. It has to be heard again and again, because its implications are always more than anyone can discern. In this letter, perhaps even more than in any other of his letters, Paul performs the task of recalling those who read it to further and further discoveries of the goodness of God towards them.

One final point may need to be made before we begin to read the text of Paul's letter in detail. Paul was dealing with a particular situation, in a particular place. He was not writing for all places and all times. It would therefore be possible to misunderstand what he wrote by taking it out of context—as though he had been speaking 'timeless truths'.

He wrote other letters, and some of them have survived. In 1 Corinthians, for example, we can see him providing instructions for congregations that were divided and confused; and he will quote the scriptures to them as laws that they must fulfil (e.g. 1 Corinthians 9:9). Similarly, he will quote instructions that go back to 'the Lord' i.e. Jesus Christ (1 Corinthians 9:14).

There have been Christians who have been totally against any kind of law. The term that describes them is 'antinomians'. Paul was not one of those. He believed that 'the whole law is summed up in a single commandment, "You shall love your neighbour as yourself"' (Galatians 5:14 quoting Leviticus 19:18).

To the Jews of the first century AD the Law of Moses was a package that had to be accepted *in toto*, without making any distinctions (see, for example, James 2:10). Paul is selective: he believes that the commandments which distinguished Jews from other people are no longer to be observed. Later writers were to make distinctions to clarify this point: the moral laws were to be observed, not the ceremonial laws—the ritual instructions, the food laws, the calendar and so on.

We are extremely fortunate in having some excellent commentaries on this letter. There is one by Martin Luther, written in the sixteenth century, that shows how the rediscovery of Paul at that time affected Christianity in the West, producing the situation of which we all are heirs.

Among the more recent commentaries, two may be picked out for mention: that of H.D. Betz, *Galatians* (Fortress, 1979); and that of J. Ziesler, *The Epistle to the Galatians* (Epworth Press, 1992).

Of older commentaries, one stands out as exceptional. Although it is based on the Greek text it can be used by those who know no Greek: E. de Witt Burton, *A Critical and Exegetical Commentary on the Epistle to the Galatians* (T. and T. Clarke, 1921). He provides at the end of the exposition (page 362) one of the best brief summaries of Galatians that has ever been written:

> *Though it was probably dictated rapidly, and was certainly composed under the stress of deep emotion, the six brief chapters of which it consists constitute one of the most important documents of early Christianity and one of the noblest pleas ever written for Christian liberty and spiritual religion.*

1 The authority of the apostle

If we had lived at the time of the Roman empire and been contemporaries of Paul we would not have signed letters at the end as we do now. We would have put our name at the beginning of a letter and it would have been the first word we wrote. This is a far more sensible way of writing letters than ours. What the reader wants to know first is whom the letter is from. There is no need to turn to the last page to find out, if the sender's name comes first. All the books of the New Testament that were originally letters begin in this way and so do the two letters that are quoted in Acts (15:23–29; 23:26–30). It was the standard procedure, used by Greeks, Romans and Jews.

Paul's letters would have been read out to the congregations to which they were addressed. So we would expect to hear the name of the writer first, then the name of the recipients (here 'the churches of Galatia') and then a greeting (here, vv. 3–5).

What is unusual in this letter is that the sender tells his correspondents not just that he is 'Paul an apostle', but what that means in his case. He writes, he says, with the authority of God and of Jesus Christ whom God raised from the dead. He is addressing (as we shall find later) people who do not agree with him and his purpose is to make them change their minds.

He has heard that they have recently started on a course of action that he believes to be totally wrong, and his aim in this letter is to persuade them to perform a complete change of direction. Moreover, it is not simply that he thinks that they are totally mistaken. He is also convinced that what they are doing now is contrary to God's will and that he has God's authority to tell them so.

It is, in fact, even stranger than that. Paul believes that he is himself part of the evidence that what the Galatian churches are now doing is a mistake. Paul's own history, his autobiography, is part of the letter, because it is an instance of the argument that he is developing. If his hearers will recall (as he will invite them to do, in chapters 1 and 2) his earlier life and the change that took place in it (his conversion) they will see that they have taken a wrong turn and that they must go back to the point where they left the right way.

Paul says what it was that they had failed to understand, and he puts it in the greeting that follows: 'grace and peace'. This is what the disagreement between Paul and the Galatians is all about: 'What is meant by God's grace (or favour) and how do we know that we have it?' 'How has God made peace with us?' Paul had already mentioned the resurrection of Jesus Christ from the dead (v. 1): that was part of the answer to the question 'How do we know about God's grace?' Now he refers to the other event by which they should have known grace and peace: the crucifixion, in which Jesus 'gave himself for our sins to set us free from the present evil age'.

The chief fault of the Galatians is that they have not yet realized the full significance of what Paul had said when he preached the gospel to them. They had believed (or so they thought) and they had been baptized. But the implications of what they were doing had been lost on them. That was why they had taken the wrong turning and why they would now have to go back.

Paul is telling them that he must recall them to the two elements that make up his gospel: Christ died for our sins and was raised for our justification.

We are 'set free from this present evil age'. This is the theme of this letter: freedom, release from prison, liberty. We are like people coming out of a dark place into the light, who can see nothing because daylight is dazzling. We grope for support, for something to hang on to. That was how it was in Galatia—and it provoked a letter from Paul that has been immensely influential throughout the history of Christianity.

PRAYER
Help us to understand your apostle and his letter.
He writes for everybody, because he knows us so well.
Show us how his gospel is good news for us.

2 Trouble-makers in Galatia

Had we been used to receiving letters from Paul we should have expected that he would here have gone on to thank God for our faith and perseverance (this, like the opening, was standard practice in the Roman empire). We should therefore have been shaken rigid on hearing the next sentence read to us in one of the Galatian churches: 'I am astonished that you are so quickly deserting the one who called you'.

Instead of thanking God for us, he is expressing his amazement at our turning our backs on God—and on doing this so soon after we had received from God his greatest gift: his Spirit, that is, his life.

We have done this by listening to people who have preached a 'different gospel' from the one that Paul preached. But it is wrong to call it a gospel, or good news. It is, Paul knows, very bad news. We had been released from prison; but now we have voluntarily accepted another prison sentence. We have put our heads into a noose.

Paul is so angry that he pronounces an anathema (a curse) on whoever led us astray. And to make it completely clear he repeats it. He would not have been happy with the attitude, 'It doesn't matter what you think or believe; it's what you do that counts.' The Galatians have allowed their minds to think strange thoughts that they had never entertained before; and these new ideas have led them to do things that they had never done in the past: 'You are observing special days, and months, and seasons, and years' (4:10). Who have done this to the Galatians and what was it that they said?

Paul never names them in this letter. He had no need, because his readers knew exactly whom he was talking about. These people had come to Galatia (after Paul had moved on) as preachers of a gospel, and they claimed that they had greater authority than that of Paul. What they said in their preaching included the requirement that Gentile believers should keep the Law of Moses that was contained in the first five books of the Hebrew scriptures (Genesis to Deuteronomy).

We shall not understand Galatians unless we see that the preachers of the different gospel in Galatia had a most persuasive case. We might well have believed them rather than Paul. They could quote scripture. God told Abraham that circumcision was to be the sign of membership of God's people for ever: 'So shall my covenant be in your flesh an everlasting covenant' (Genesis 17:13, but see the whole chapter).

The Jewish martyrs who had died in the wars against the Greeks two centuries before had given up their lives rather than break the food laws by eating unclean meat (2 Maccabees 7). Jesus had been circumcised and had attended synagogue services. He had said that he had not come to abolish the Law or the Prophets (Matthew 5:17). The headquarters church of the Christian movement, in Jerusalem, was led by James the Lord's brother and the family of Jesus were members of it (Acts 1:14). They all kept the Law. In any case, if charity 'beareth all things' should not the Gentile believers put up with some inconvenience in order to preserve the unity of the churches? Jesus had not made it clear whether his followers should cease to live as Jews.

Those who preached this other gospel were welcomed by the churches of Galatia: they were willing to keep the Law, beginning with the liturgical calendar. The trouble-makers may have said (rightly or wrongly) that they came with the knowledge and authority of the church in Jerusalem to make up the deficiencies of the churches established by Paul. Paul, we shall see, emphasizes his independence of Jerusalem. He had no need of any human commission, because he was sent by God through Jesus Christ. People who came from James had caused trouble in Antioch (2:12) and it may have been similar preachers who had started the movement for keeping the Law in Galatia.

Quarrels among Christians and divisions between churches are not recent. Nor are they necessarily signs of our latter-day degeneration. They were there from the earliest Christian history. This letter may have been written within twenty-five years of the resurrection. Paul's letters to Corinth, Rome and Philippi also show the existence of groups among the churches who opposed one another—each claiming that it alone had the true gospel. God limits himself to what we can manage. He deals with us through human beings. His witnesses are flesh and blood and they are not without sin. They retain their ambitions, their quarrelsomeness, and their fear of people with ideas different from their own. All their insights are partial and imperfect.

PRAYER

Forgive us our trespasses.
Thank you for accepting us as we are.
Do your will in spite of us.

19

3 The limits of diversity

It has often been said that reading the New Testament letters (especially those written by Paul) is like listening to a telephone conversation when you can only hear what one party is saying. In order to make sense of what is going on you have to work out for yourself what the other person must have said, and it is always possible to make a mistake.

When Paul asks, rhetorically, 'Am I now seeking human approval?' he is probably replying to people in Galatia who were accusing him of acting merely in order to win popularity and support and saying that he lacked principles. They might well have had evidence (of a kind) to make such a charge against him, because Paul himself says that when he was with Jews he lived like a Jew and when he was with Gentiles he lived like a Gentile: 'I have become all things to all people.' He explains why: 'That I might by all means save some' (1 Corinthians 9:19–23).

Paul believed that the question of Jewish lifestyle was now a matter of the past and that it could be treated with indifference. All that mattered now was preaching the gospel and faith in God. He must preach, and he must do it in the way that he believed it had to be done—which was not how his opponents in Galatia were doing it. He believed that God had revealed to him the truth of the gospel and that he had appointed him as an apostle (that is, 'one sent') to preach this to the Gentiles.

He had no choice in the matter. He was a slave of Christ and slaves had no freedom to choose. They had to do what they were told. So he is understandably angry that his missionary strategy of adopting the customs of those with whom he is living (over such matters as sabbath-observance, food regulations, attendance at synagogue and so on) is being interpreted as lack of principle and attributed to a low motive. They are using it as a stick to beat him and as a way of blackening his reputation in the churches that he has founded in Galatia.

'Am I now seeking human approval?' he asks. The letter that he is writing shows that this cannot be so. *Now*, in what he has just written in this letter, he has shown that there are limits to what can be approved of in the churches. His opponents have gone beyond the limits. That is why he has said, twice over for emphasis, 'let them be accursed!'

We often ask the questions: 'Where are the boundaries of the church?' 'What is the minimum that must be believed?' 'How do we know whether somebody is a Christian or not?' 'Are there tests for membership of the church?' The letter to the Galatians gives us one answer to these problems. Total contradiction cannot be legitimate. Paul gives an example in another letter; no one who was inspired by the Spirit could say both 'Jesus is Lord' and 'let Jesus be cursed!' (1 Corinthians 12:3); the first is the complete opposite of the second.

The same idea lies at the root of much of what he says here in this letter to the Galatians. Either God is dealing with us through the Law that he gave to Moses or he is not. Either we are right with God through keeping the Law (circumcision, food laws, sabbaths, etc.) or those things no longer matter.

As his letter proceeds we shall see more and more examples of this either/or method of argument. Paul, who was a large-hearted and intelligent and peace-loving person—even he could not find a way of containing in one community people who had totally opposite views; that is, both those who insisted that everybody keep the Law and those who believed that the former rules no longer applied. Later on, when he wrote to the Christians in Rome, he did his best to accommodate both sides. But that was because those who stood out for keeping the Law might, he hoped, no longer insist that others should do so.

In Galatia, he believes, there is less willingness on the part of the pro-Law trouble-makers to come to any arrangement with the others, short of enforcing their total submission. Therefore, if that was their agenda, the only solution was to bar them from the churches. That is what this letter aims to do.

PRAYER

Let us not misrepresent those with whom we disagree.
Help us to see where we must take a stand.
Give us the courage to speak boldly when we should.

4 Gospel means message

The word 'gospel' is important in this letter. Paul has already used it twice, in verses 6 and 7, and it will come seven times in all. There is also an associated word meaning 'to preach the gospel' and it comes six times. The words were characteristic of Paul—some of his favourite expressions. To us, 'gospel' suggests a book: the four Gospels, or the apocryphal Gospels of Philip, Thomas, and so on. But none of these had been written when Paul was using the word, so it would not have made the recipients of the letter think of a book. It meant a message. And not just any message, but one that you would be glad to hear. It meant good news.

In one of his later letters Paul will say more about the message. It is good news about Jesus, his death and resurrection and the significance of these events for everyone (1 Corinthians 15:3–5). He says there that he had received it and he must mean that he had received it from those who were believers before him. Here, however, he emphasizes something different: 'the gospel that was proclaimed by me is not of human origin; for I did not receive it from a human source.'

To the Corinthians he says he has received it. To the Galatians he says he had not. It looks as though he is contradicting himself. But that is not so. It is one thing to hear words spoken by human beings. It is something entirely different to believe what you hear. Believing requires more than simply hearing; faith comes from God.

The distinction between hearing and believing goes back to a passage in Isaiah that is quoted frequently in the New Testament:

> *Keep listening but do not comprehend; keep looking but do not under-*
> *stand. Make the mind of this people dull, and stop their ears, and shut*
> *their eyes, so that they may not look with their eyes, and listen with their*
> *ears, and comprehend with their minds, and turn and be healed.*

Isaiah 6:9–10

It is a common experience that you can hear without understanding and see without grasping the point. The penny does not drop.

Paul had been listening to what the followers of Jesus were saying for some time before he believed it for himself. That was why he had persecuted the church. He had thought that what they said was blasphemous, because it involved saying things about Jesus, a human being, that no good Jew could ever say.

Paul changed from being a persecutor to being a follower—and the change was not the result of anything done by a human being. It was the work of God (see v. 15). God had shown Paul who Jesus was and what Jesus was doing. So though Paul had listened to people preaching the gospel he had not comprehended it. And though he had looked at the disciples he had not understood who they were. His understanding, comprehension and faith all came from God— not from a human source.

Galatians is about a conflict within the fellowship of Christ's disciples. Both sides of the conflict agree in some respects and disagree in others—and the disagreement runs very deep and has become extremely bitter. We have only Paul's side of the argument, and he is saying of anyone who opposes him from the other side, 'let that one be accursed!' No doubt his opponents said the same of him. They agreed, however, on the events that constituted the gospel: Jesus had died, and God had raised him to life, and he had been seen after the resurrection. They agreed also that the scriptures had been fulfilled. Where they disagreed was over the implications of these things: was it now the case that Gentiles did not have to keep the Law of Moses in the way that Jews had done in the past?

Paul believes that his opponents in Galatia have not yet seen this necessary implication of the gospel—and he believes that it was God who revealed it to him. The trouble in Galatia was an example of a situation in which that the Christian church sometimes finds itself in. There is more to the gospel than we or our predecessors had thought. So perhaps there may be aspects of it still waiting to be perceived; implications not yet uncovered. The process of revealing the truth of the gospel to those who are already believers (but have not yet seen what is involved) is painful, both for those with insight and for those who lack it. There is no avoiding the pain.

PRAYER

Forgive our blindness and inertia.
Sustain our prophets and teachers.
Help us to comprehend and understand.

5 Paul, a man sent by God

At the beginning of the letter Paul had said that he was an apostle 'sent neither by human commission nor from human authorities, but through Jesus Christ and God the Father' (v. 1). He returns to that, now, to show that this must be true. He is emphasizing it because there are people in Galatia who are saying that Paul must have received his authority from others—presumably, from the Jerusalem apostles. He must therefore be inferior to them. They would point to the fact that Paul had not been a follower of Jesus before the crucifixion, and they could argue from this that in any conflict between what the Jerusalem apostles said and what Paul said they must be preferred; because they were superior to him. This is what Paul is disputing here. He and his message, he is saying, both come directly from Jesus Christ. The evidence for this is his autobiography.

There was a complete break in his life and a total change of direction. Up to a certain point he was going one way but after that he was going in the opposite way. He had disapproved of the followers of Jesus and tried to stamp the movement out. What motivated him at that time was zeal for the Law. He was a Pharisee—one of those who took the Law extremely seriously. (It should be noted that persecution of Jews by Jews was rare in the first century and that it would be a mistake to think of them as at all like Christians of later ages. Groups of Jews holding conflicting views, such as on resurrection, could co-exist side by side without resorting to violence.)

Then God intervened. Paul had thought that Jesus was a blasphemer who had rightly been executed by crucifixion and shown by the authorities to be cursed by God. He had also thought that the followers of Jesus participated in his error. Now, as a result of God's intervention, Jesus has been revealed to him as God's Son, his agent who does his Father's will. Paul also believed that he must preach this gospel to the Gentiles. In what order these ideas came to Paul he does not pause to tell us. The main point he wants to make is that this happened.

The persecutor became the apostle to the Gentiles—and it all happened without the intervention or assistance of any human beings. (Paul does not say anything about the part played by Ananias who is mentioned in Acts 9:10–19.) Paul did not go to Jerusalem—nor did he join any other group of believers. He went to Arabia—to preach—and then returned to Damascus, where his conversion had taken place. (See 2 Corinthians 11:32f. for Paul's account of his escape from Damascus. He was a wanted man because of what he was saying and he was already regarded as a trouble-maker.)

Paul's autobiography stresses the intervention of God in his life. It was God who had 'set him apart before he was born' (compare Isaiah 49:1) and 'called him' (to be an apostle) 'through his grace' (not because he deserved it: he had been a persecutor. 'Grace' is another key word in this letter). Paul was a persecutor before he had contact with those 'who were already apostles before him'. There could not have been any opportunity for anyone to give authority to Paul— except God. The facts show that he is a man sent by God.

This passage underlines the priority of God in the life of Paul. The change of direction, from Pharisee to apostle, only makes sense if it is the action of God. And in the circumstances there was no one else involved. God acted alone. There is some sort of parallel to this kind of writing (theological autobiography) in the Old Testament prophets: Amos, Hosea, Jeremiah and Ezekiel all had initiatory visions which they record. A classic of this kind of writing, three hundred years later, is Augustine's *Confessions*, in which he shows how his life was directed and controlled by God. Writing of this sort seems to be characteristic of the Jewish-Christian tradition and to depend on a belief about God and his relationship with the individual believer.

Throughout this letter Paul will appeal to facts that could be checked: his conversion; his first visit to the Galatians; their faith and the gift of the Spirit; their freedom from previous restraints; the harvest of the Spirit; the marks on Paul's body, which showed that what he said was unacceptable to those who kept the Law of Moses.

Christianity is not simply a matter of faith. There is evidence— and some of this evidence is accessible to everybody. Believers have the testimony themselves. Loss of faith is a kind of self-contradiction.

PRAYER

Thank you for bringing us to this moment in our lives:
for everything that has led up to the present;
for those who have taught us and influenced us;
for gifts and graces freely given to us; for your knowledge of us.

6
Praise God for Paul

Paul continues to assert his independence. He was not instructed by anyone except God. He certainly wasn't instructed by the church in Jerusalem. The first time he went back there (after his conversion) was three years later, and he met Cephas, that is, Peter. (Paul refers to him more frequently by this Aramaic word, 'Cephas' meaning 'Rock', than by the Greek word 'Peter'.) He explains that he only stayed for a fortnight and that the only other apostle that he met was James, the Lord's brother, who seems to have become the leader of the Jerusalem church.

Paul insists, with an oath, that this is the truth—presumably because people were putting around a different story which implied that Paul had been instructed by the church in Jerusalem and that he was deviating from what he had been taught by them. No one else met him. They only heard that he had become a preacher of the gospel—and they gave thanks to God for him.

Paul skilfully puts key words that express his side of the argument into the mouths of the members of the Judean churches—people whom one might have expected to have been on the side of his opponents. They said that Paul was now 'proclaiming the faith'; literally: preaching as good news the faith he once tried to destroy. Paul makes them speak in his language and adds that they glorified God because of Paul. They, unlike his opponents in Galatia, realized that God was at work in Paul. If preaching the faith was a reason for glorifying God then, why is he being condemned for doing it now? Paul is claiming that the trouble-makers lack consistency.

He says that for three years after his conversion he never went back to Jerusalem. Why would this be? Was it because he was too embarrassed to meet the families and friends of those he had killed? Or was he afraid of the Jewish authorities in Jerusalem, whom he might well have expected to treat him badly as a traitor who had changed sides? He gives us no reason for his absence from Jerusalem and the delay in returning there. We wonder why he did not go back at least briefly to 'clear his desk' and settle up with his landlady.

The only conclusion he wants us to draw is that what had happened to him in Damascus had convinced him that God meant him to preach the gospel to Gentiles. That is what he went to Arabia to do, and then to Damascus and 'the regions of Syria and Cilicia', instead of returning to Jerusalem—except for one fortnight, and that only after three years, when he saw no more than two of the leaders of the church there. He would not build on another's foundations; nor did he need instruction from predecessors. He was doing what he believed he had been called by God to do and he was getting on with it without delay.

It is understandable. If one was suddenly, unexpectedly, and completely convinced that what one had been doing was utterly mistaken and that what one should be doing was the opposite—and that this had been shown to one by God himself—then the most obvious reaction would be to begin the new life immediately. Without any delay, and without even returning to apologise and ask for forgiveness.

Paul declared his change of mind by his immediate change of direction—from destroyer of the church to the one who built it up. The churches of Judea recognized what had happened, he says, and praised God for his conversion.

PRAYER
Make us see your will as what we must do, immediately.
Give us a sense of urgency.
May you be glorified because of us.

7 Paul fights for our freedom

Paul continues his brief and selective autobiography. His purpose is to demonstrate his independence of all other Christian groups, particularly the church in Jerusalem. His reason for doing this is that people in Galatia are saying that Paul is wrong and that the Jerusalem church is right. They keep the Law of Moses, he does not. Paul's argument is that he is dependent on God for what he says; therefore he must be believed.

He begins now (2:1) to describe his next visit to Jerusalem, the second after his conversion (and, as far as he says in this letter, the only other time that he went there, before writing to the Galatians). In Acts 15 there is an account of a meeting in Jerusalem at which Paul was present. It is probably a different version of the occasion which Paul is describing here, told more from the side of those who disagreed with him. The Acts' account is sometimes described as the Council of Jerusalem and Paul is presented as answering hostile questions to those in authority. Paul's version of the event puts a different light on it. He tells the Galatians what happened in a way that shows that he was answerable to no one except God. The second visit was fourteen years *after*—either after his conversion or after the first visit. He is not, therefore, one who must constantly report back to a higher authority in Jerusalem. He did not go alone; Barnabas and Titus went with him. Both of them will be mentioned further on (vv. 3, 13), and the reason for referring to them may be that Paul wants to show that he alone stood out for the truth of the gospel.

He did not go simply by his own choice, nor was he summoned by the church in Jerusalem to come up and explain himself to them. He went because of a revelation, that is, in response to God. He gives no further explanation of this but his motive is clear. He is not in a position to be called upon by others to give an account of his ministry. Any discussion of his preaching was only at a private meeting— not before a plenary session of the whole church in Jerusalem. He had taken part in this discussion so that what he was doing in his ministry might not be destroyed by others; might not be 'in vain'.

He had in fact been trying to prevent a situation like that which had developed in Galatia, where trouble-makers were saying that the Jerusalem church was the model for all other churches and that the Law of Moses was to be kept by Gentile Christians. The reference to Titus is ambiguous: does Paul mean that it was not required that Titus be circumcised, so he was not; or that he was circumcised, though the Jerusalem church did not require it? Whichever he meant, Paul refers to the subject because others had used it as a case in point. They said that it proved that they were right. Paul denies this.

Paul's purpose, he says, was to maintain freedom for Gentile believers, in the face of false Christians who wanted to bring them into slavery; he was doing this for the sake of his present readers in Galatia (*you*), that they might be free.

Paul introduces words and ideas that will play an important part in the argument as he sets it out in the rest of this letter. The terms he uses are slavery and freedom, ideas that would be immediately understood in the Roman empire when everybody was either a slave or a free person. Galatians is a plea for Christian liberty. It contains more than a third of all the instances of the word 'freedom' in the New Testament, and more than a quarter of the instances of the adjective 'free'.

What enslaves us in religion is fear of irrational taboos and superstitions; prohibitions create a sense of guilt in those who break them, or who live in terror that they may. The gospel releases those who are threatened by such fears.

Mark, whose Gospel is closest to the insights of Paul, presents Jesus as one who taught that all food was clean and that what defiled was what came from within (from the heart) not anything that entered from without (7:1–23).

Thank God for Paul! He has delivered us from fear of things that we have no reason to fear: the number thirteen; walking under ladders; a single magpie; the predictions of astrologers; things to do with colour, race and sex. Magic was a thriving industry in the first century AD and Christianity was its enemy. In Matthew's Gospel the magicians worshipped Christ—and they handed over the tools of their trade and the money they made by it.

PRAYER

Thank you for the gospel.
Thank you for freedom from fear and superstition.
Thank you for all who have defied the irrational in the name of Christ.

Gospel not tradition

In Jerusalem, as later in Galatia, Paul was faced with people who had not realized the implications of what they believed. The gospel is the enemy of superstition, the arbitrary and the taboo (which includes much of what was commanded and prohibited in the Law of Moses). It also refuses to be stifled by tradition. What was the case in the past may be so no longer and every appeal to antiquity has to be scrutinized in the light of freedom and universality. Paul is explaining this in these three verses (6–8) and the significance of them is vast.

His account of his second visit to Jerusalem is told in such a way that it will answer a question that was to arise later, in Galatia. People in Galatia will say, 'How can Paul be right and the Jerusalem church leaders wrong over such an important issue as the keeping of the Law of God? How can anyone think that those who were with Jesus in the days of his flesh were mistaken and are still in the dark? Must they not be closer to the truth than a man who did not know Jesus then and who says himself that he had very little contact with them later?'

It is the argument from tradition, against anything that is seen to be an innovation, and it has always had great potency in religious matters. Paul is here rejecting it.

Why are there 'acknowledged leaders'? He must be referring to Cephas/Peter and to James, among others. Simon had been given the nickname Cephas, 'Rock', by Jesus—but Paul did not draw the conclusion from this that everything Peter did was right. (He will demonstrate this in verses 11–14, below) James was the Lord's brother—but that relationship did not guarantee his authority, Paul says.

He gives his reason. What they were, in the past, makes no difference to Paul, in the present; because God is no respecter of persons (as the Law itself says in Deuteronomy 10:17). God is not bound by the past. He raised Jesus from the dead (1:1) and he can deliver us from restrictions and limitations, even from matters that are as close to Paul and his readers as the events in the life of Jesus. (Once again, Mark's Gospel illustrates the same idea: 'Who are my mother and my brothers?' 3:33). God can initiate new beginnings; he has done so, in the case of Paul himself.

The leaders of the Jerusalem church, Paul says, 'contributed nothing' to him. They did not add anything to what Paul had, by then, been preaching for at least fourteen years. They did not insist that he went back to all the churches he had founded and tell them all to keep the Law of Moses. On the contrary, they agreed that God was working through Paul in churches where the Law was not observed, just as he was working through Peter in churches where the Law was being observed.

You could recognize the activity of the same God in both cases. It was the same Jesus who was preached, the same death and resurrection; the same Spirit was received and the same miracles followed. God was not restricted by uniformity. He could be seen as the lover of variety, empowering Peter for a ministry to those who continued to keep the Law, and empowering Paul for a ministry to those who did not.

The extraordinary importance of the letter to the Galatians is that it is evidence for the change within the first generation of a movement that began as a subdivision of Judaism, into something that did not remain within that original setting and culture. The ugly duckling has turned into a swan. It never was a duckling—and now it has grown up it is seen for what it really is.

PRAY

Give us ears to hear.
Teach us to let go of the past.
Give us courage.

9 Grace to recognize grace

Paul's account of his second visit to Jerusalem and of the meetings that took place at that time, ends with the statement that James, Cephas and John acknowledged that God was at work in Paul. James, the Lord's brother is mentioned first—perhaps because he had become the overall leader of the church in Jerusalem. Cephas is Peter, and John is one of the sons of Zebedee. (This recognition was similar to what happened in Judea, when the churches there glorified God because of Paul after his first visit to Jerusalem.)

Paul was to go to the Gentiles, and they would go to the Jews. The only request they made of Paul was not that he should teach his converts to keep the Law of Moses but only that Paul and those who were associated with him should 'remember the poor', that is, the believers in Judea and Jerusalem. This was something that Paul was already eager to do. (We know that he fulfilled this instruction because he refers to 'the collection for the saints', in Romans 15:25-29; 1 Corinthians 16:1-4, and 2 Corinthians 8 and 9.)

If, therefore the trouble-makers in Galatia are saying that they have the authority of the church in Jerusalem, either they are lying, or the leaders in Jerusalem have forgotten what was decided, or they have subsequently changed their minds. Paul's argument is that he was doing in Galatia what had been agreed in Jerusalem. Paul was recognized as partner with the Jerusalem leaders. (The word Paul uses is from the same group as the word used of another James and his brother John in Luke 5:10—they 'were partners with Simon' in the fishing industry.) Shaking hands was a symbolic act expressing fellowship, partnership.

If, as many think, this meeting is the same as that described in Acts 15, there are obvious differences between Paul's account of it and Luke's. In the latter, an agreement is reached about what may have been minimum regulations for ritual purity to be expected of the Gentiles. Paul says nothing about this either here or elsewhere. But in any case, what is surprising is that both accounts, Paul's and Luke's, agree that circumcision was not required of Gentile converts.

This is remarkable. What had already been stated as a law for all generations in scripture (Genesis 17) was now no longer accepted as necessary for all members of the people of God, the seed of Abraham. Jesus is believed to be 'the end of the law' (Romans 10:4) in the sense that observance of some laws now ceases to be necessary. The Law-keeping church in Jerusalem had agreed to that. It must have taken some grace to do so.

It takes grace to recognize grace. It takes the Spirit of God to release us from our good and helpful religious traditions when they have become a hindrance to what God is about to do. God is not trapped by the past, but is always dragging his people forward, releasing them from restrictions that may have been useful at one time but have now ceased to serve his purpose. The direction in which he is moving is always towards greater freedom and diversity with less uniformity. Without grace we hang on to the past and reject the liberty that he is offering us.

PRAYER

Release us from what holds us back.
Give us grace to recognize your grace.
Demolish us and rebuild us.

10 Paul rebukes Peter

Paul moves on now from the account of his second visit to Jerusalem to the next incident in his summary of the past. In Antioch (in Syria) an arrangement had been reached whereby the whole church, both those who had been Jews and those who had been Gentiles before their conversion, joined in one common meal. Paul and Barnabas were there when Cephas arrived and at first he joined in this practice of eating with the Gentiles. But he changed his mind when a group of Jewish-Christians from Jerusalem arrived—possibly sent by James the Lord's brother in order to make sure that what was happening in Antioch could have the approval of the church in Jerusalem.

Whatever the reason for their coming to Antioch, their arrival and Peter's withdrawal from the common meal caused a crisis in the church in Antioch. It divided into two: Jewish Christians, (including Barnabas, Paul's assistant) against the Gentile Christians.

Paul believed that one of the implications of the gospel was that Christ had died for everybody. Everybody had sinned, but now there was one act of righteousness that put everybody, equally, right with God. The distinction between Jews and Gentiles had been abolished (Romans 3:21–31). Therefore, to Paul, what the Jewish-Christians were doing was not consistent 'with the truth of the gospel'.

He addressed Cephas, but he spoke to him 'before them all'. Cephas had changed his practice, therefore he was the obvious target for Paul's rebuke. His influence, no doubt, had contributed to the action of the other Jewish-Christians in departing from the common meal. But what Cephas had done was in fact worse than that, because Paul assumed (without saying it explicitly) that there can only be one common meal in the church. If there were two—one for ex-Jews and another for ex-Gentiles—neither would be the common meal.

Therefore, if Peter is insisting on the observation of Jewish food laws in the meal, he is now compelling ex-Gentiles to 'live like Jews'. He had formerly lived like a Gentile himself, before the people from Jerusalem arrived; but now he has given that up. What sort of faith in the truth of the gospel is this?

It looks as though the agreement that had been reached in Jerusalem, that Paul described in the previous verses (2:7–10), had been made without anyone foreseeing the problems that would arise in a mixed congregation. Peter could go to Jews, Paul could to Gentiles, and all would be well if their converts never met. The Jewish believers could continue to keep the Law and the Gentile believers need not. The situation in Antioch provoked an unexpected crisis.

'The truth of the gospel' is always waiting to burst out on us. It is like a time-bomb that can go off at any moment. When it does go off, it demolishes assumptions and practices that we have adopted without question concerning (for example) class or colour or sex. Peter is reasserting the pre-Christian ideas of Judaism, so he needs Paul to 'oppose him to his face'.

We only have Paul's side of the argument. No doubt there were those who would have said that Paul needed Peter: tradition and the past must not be completely abandoned. Paul would have agreed. He continued to study the scriptures and he did not, like Marcion in the second century, reject the Old Testament as irrelevant to Christianity.

Peter needs Paul to rebuke him and Paul needs Peter to express the need for tradition, continuity, the wisdom of the past, God's revelation of himself in former times. The activity of the church is always an educational process and it requires people with different gifts and personalities to uphold and preserve the necessary traditions. No one person has the whole truth. God works through a variety of gifts and the mutual contradictions and disagreements of individuals. Paul was to say so, later, to the Corinthians: 'There have to be factions [literally: heresies] among you, for only so will it become clear who among you are genuine' (1 Corinthians 11:19).

PRAYER

Teach us to oppose what is inconsistent with the gospel.
Make us willing to be rebuked.
Move us all towards greater understanding of the truth.

11 Not by works but by faith

The remaining verses of chapter 2 (15–21) are an elucidation of what Paul meant when he opposed Cephas in Antioch. When Paul has completed this part of the letter he will immediately deal with the situation in Galatia: 'You foolish Galatians!' (3:1).

What has happened in Galatia is a repetition of what had happened earlier in Antioch. The foolish Galatians are making the same mistake as Peter: they are going back on the freedom they had begun to practise in order to keep customs and regulations that are now out of date. The gospel has made the Law antiquated. To attempt to revive it is to be a renegade.

Paul says 'we ourselves' (he and Peter and Barnabas and all other Jews who have become believers), have changed their minds. Previously they used to think that being right with God involved them in keeping the Law as set out in scripture. But now they no longer think that this is so. Instead of keeping the laws what matters now is Jesus Christ. He has assured them of God's approval of them. This relationship between Jesus Christ and these former Jews, what it is that has changed their minds and the way they live, is called *faith*.

At this point in his letter Paul is setting up with all the clarity that he can muster the contrast between obedience to the Law of Moses (which he calls 'works of the Law' and which includes circumcision, food laws, sabbath observance) and 'faith in Christ' (which excludes obedience to the Law). This is not a contrast between doing something and doing nothing, as though Jews were active and believers were inactive. It is a contrast between two levels of activity. Above all, the Law requires you to separate yourself from those who do not keep it (see 2:12: Peter 'drew back and kept himself separate'). But Christ and faith in him involve no such practices. The way of Christ, Paul will say, is 'through love to become slaves to one another' (5:13). There is no limit to this, but complete freedom: Christ died for all.

How did Paul know that no one will be justified by keeping the Law? He knew it from his experience of keeping the Law, and of being 'far more zealous for the traditions of my ancestors' than any of his contemporaries (1:14). That had led him to persecute the church of God and try to destroy it (1:13). On one side of the contrast were Law and the destruction of the church; on the other side were faith and being right with God. Works of the Law and faith were therefore mutually exclusive alternatives. You could either keep the Law and be God's enemy (as Paul had been) or you could be a believer in Christ and be right with God.

Peter had abandoned the Law (of clean and unclean food) at Antioch, until people came from Jerusalem. Then he had changed his mind. He decided that what he was doing was against God's will and that it was sin. So he had gone back to keeping the Law, taking all the ex-Jews with him except Paul. He was declaring publicly that what he had done in faith (eating with Gentiles) was sinful. He was, therefore, Paul says, making out that Christ, in whom he had believed, had led him into sin. (The NRSV translation: 'a servant of sin' is not as good as the REB translation: a 'promoter of sin'.)

Paul is using the kind of argument called *reductio ad absurdum*; hence his denial of the conclusion: 'Certainly not!' The validity of the argument here depends on the assumption that it was Christ who had led Peter to join the common meal at Antioch in the first place. Peter could reply to Paul that he (Peter) had been mistaken and that Christ had not intended him to do this.

Paul is so convinced of the implication of the gospel and of Christ as the end of the Law that he does not pause to reflect that Peter may not have shared his clarity on this matter. He had attributed Peter's changes of action to *fear*—'fear of the circumcision faction' (2:12). Fear and faith are opposites (see Mark 5:36: 'Do not fear, only believe').

PRAYER

Let us not be afraid of our freedom.
Thank you for our justification.
Thank you for faith.

12
He loved me

As Paul comes to the end of his account of events in the past he returns to the point at which he had begun. He had been a zealous Jew who persecuted the church—until God intervened, revealing his Son to him (1:13–17). God had transferred him from one side to the other. It was like death and resurrection.

'Through the law I died to the law'. Keeping the Law made him condemn Jesus and his followers as blasphemers. But when God revealed who Jesus was Paul immediately saw the Law as out of date and knew himself to be released from it. But it was God who was the cause of the change in Paul. Therefore, when he 'died to the law', the alternative was to 'live to God'.

The antithesis is very bold, since Jews and trouble-makers in Galatia and the foolish Galatians who believed the trouble-makers would all say that the Law was the Law of God. Paul, on the other hand, is saying that the Law is the opposite of God and that God is the opposite of the Law—and that he had experienced this in his own life.

He then takes up a metaphor to express this change from death to life. Jesus had died by the Roman method of executing slaves— crucifixion. God had raised him to life. Paul, like other New Testament writers, does not say of Jesus, *He lived and died* but always *He died and lives* (see, for example, Romans 6:10). The life of Jesus followed his death and began on the day of his resurrection. In the same way, Paul's life (in the real sense) began after his conversion, which was like crucifixion and resurrection. The old came to an end and the new began. (When Paul is writing to the Romans, in chapter 6, he will remind them that their initiation into the church was by baptism and that the meaning of the action was sharing in Christ's death and resurrection to a new life.)

But it is more than a change of circumstances or of manner of life. It is not just that Paul has stopped keeping the Law and adopted a Law-free lifestyle. Paul has died and someone else is now living in Paul. When he said, 'They glorified God because of me' (1:24), the Greek could have been translated, 'They glorified God in me.' God had taken over and Paul was the place in which he was working. Similarly here: 'It is no longer I who live, but it is Christ who lives in me.'

He explains what this means. His present life (in 'the flesh', which will last until Christ returns and flesh and blood are changed into spirit and glory) is lived 'by faith', and faith is union with Christ to such a degree that the actions performed by Paul are really the actions of Christ.

Paul has come to this understanding of himself through his reflection on the gospel and on what God has revealed to him of its meaning. Jesus chose to die: it was an event which he willed to happen. He did it, Paul believes, for the sake of everybody and its effect was universal. One died for all, therefore all were dead. And he did this because he loved all—there could be no other reason. Paul had never known Jesus before the crucifixion. But Jesus knew Paul, and 'loved' him, and 'gave himself' up to death for him.

It was a one-sided thing to do. That is what *grace* is. It is God being *for* people, Christ dying for people who are sinners, weak, his enemies. The Law, on the other hand, requires obedience. Christ's love and God's are unilateral, entirely independent of the response of those who are loved. To return to keeping the Law, and think that one's status as right with God (i.e. 'justification' or 'righteousness'; it is the same word in Greek) depended on obedience to the Law (as Paul had done before his conversion, as Peter was doing at Antioch after the arrival of the people from James, and as the foolish Galatians are doing now), is to make nothing of 'the grace of God'. It is to reject the offer of a free gift and insist on paying for it.

PRAYER

Make us understand that we are loved.
Overcome our reluctance to receive your gifts.
Stop us from justifying ourselves.

GALATIANS 3:1-5

Was it the Law or the gospel?

Paul has been inviting the Galatians to reflect on what has happened. He began with his life before his conversion and after; then the two visits to Jerusalem; then the incident at Antioch. All through, the argument has been that God works through faith in Christ without the keeping of the Law. But up to this point the events he has referred to have been occasions in which the Galatians themselves were not involved. Now, however, he argues from a fact within their own experience.

There is one thing they cannot possibly deny: they did receive the Spirit. There was a day when something happened, and they all understood it to be the coming of the Spirit into the Christian community in Galatia. Paul does not describe it, because he had no need to: they all knew what he was talking about. It was a day no one could forget, similar to our 'What were you doing when you heard that President Kennedy had ben shot or that Margaret Thatcher would not stand for re-election?' It was probably marked by supernatural events—speaking with tongues, prophesying, healings and miracles.

What happened to assure them that they had received the Spirit was not in question: what was to be considered was what they were doing at the time. This is 'the only thing' that they need to reflect upon. Were they doing the works of the Law (circumcising baby boys, keeping the sabbath, observing food laws, as all Jews should?) or what were they doing?

The answer had to be, 'They were listening to Paul as he preached the gospel of the dying and rising Christ'. Faith came through hearing and what was heard was the good news about the death and resurrection of Jesus.

But notice that Paul says: 'It was *before your eyes* that Jesus Christ was publicly exhibited as crucified'—not: *in your hearing*. He will come back to his first visit to Galatia in the next chapter and he will say there that it was because of sickness of some kind that he first preached to them. This was a temptation for them to scorn him. But they did not: they welcomed him as Christ Jesus.

In the world in which Paul lived the expectation would be that the agent of a god would be taken care of by his lord: he would not be sick or accident-prone or experience any sort of failure (4:13–15). But the Galatians did not despise Paul or reject his message: they saw in this sick man the agent of the crucified Saviour, and miraculously they believed and received the Spirit.

How foolish they are, then, to go on now to keep the Law with its regulations. He dismisses these matters as 'flesh' in order to contrast them with the Spirit. By the Spirit God had incorporated the believers into his own life; they were partakers in the existence of God. They could not have more than that. Why ever, then, begin to keep the Law?

The way their Christian life began is the key to understanding how it will go on. It began with something coming out of the blue, without any fulfilment of preconditions. It was sheer grace, gift, bonanza. This sick man stood up and talked, and God took over; that was it. That is how it will be, always: everything depends on God, who is always ahead of his servants, going before them, initiating their good works, pouring his goodness upon them, freely. Not waiting for any response, but making response possible by the gift of faith.

We have the evidence in ourselves. We are his handiwork, the product of his grace. Just as we did not ask to be born, so we did not ask to be born again. We did nothing to qualify. It is all grace. Paul's argument is that if we remember how it is with us we shall understand the ways of God: we can read them off from our own experience.

PRAYER

We did nothing to earn your grace.
While we were enemies, we were reconciled to God.
We received the Spirit without asking.

14 Descendants of Abraham

The character of Paul's letter changes here. So far it has been mainly autobiographical, but now it becomes expository. Between 3:6 and 5:1 Paul will quote and comment on at least a dozen passages of scripture. His purpose is to show that he is not being anti-scriptural in not requiring Gentile believers to keep the Law; scripture itself is on his side. We must suppose that he is answering his opponents, who also will have quoted scripture in support of their contention that Gentile Christians should be circumcised and live as Jews. They have therefore determined which passages should be used—and the institution of circumcision at the time of Abraham was an obvious example. Paul begins his expository section here by taking up texts from Genesis in which God's dealings with Abraham were recorded.

As we have seen already (in the Introduction) when it came to scripture the opponents had the better case. Paul's argument depends more on what has happened recently than on what had happened in the past. That may be why he puts autobiography before exposition of scripture in the letter. He believes that the real meaning of the Law is only seen by those who 'turn to the Lord' (2 Corinthians 3:16). Gospel, faith, conversion, baptism and the gift of the Spirit all come first. Then, after that, the reading of scripture, which will reveal its truth to those who, through faith, already know what it is they are looking for.

Who are the descendants of Abraham? This was the question that the row in Galatia raised. Paul's opponents said it was those who were circumcised. Paul says it is those who have faith. They could appeal to Genesis 17; he appeals to an earlier chapter in Genesis, namely 15:6. (The word 'believed' in Greek is the verb that is formed from the word 'faith': there is no difference in Greek, between 'faith' and 'belief'; or between 'having faith' and 'believing'.)

Paul has another passage from Genesis (12:3, also 18:18) to show that God had foretold the blessing of the non-Jewish nations (i.e. the Gentiles) in, or by, Abraham. What was it, therefore, that Abraham had and the Gentiles might have also? Not circumcision and the rest of the Law; if they adopted that, they would no longer be Gentiles. Gentiles would be blessed by having faith, in exactly the same way that Abraham had faith.

Paul does not explain at this point in his letter what is meant by 'faith'; he does not describe the content of faith. He will do that later, when he writes to the Romans (chapter 4), perhaps because people had asked him to explain how Abraham's faith could be reproduced in Gentiles now. Both, he says, believe in God who raises the dead: Abraham believed that God could give a son to a couple who were as good as dead; Christians believe that God raised his Son from the dead. But here, in Galatians, he is content to argue by means of words that are not well defined or given any specific content, 'faith', 'righteousness' and 'blessing'. They derive their meaning from the context in which they are used. Who are the descendants of Abraham? Those who have faith; they are the righteous; God's blessing is on them. All this was established in Genesis 12 and 15 before there was any mention of circumcision and 430 years before the Law was given (see notes on Galatians 3:17).

It is almost inevitable that in any association of men and women somebody will want to define the boundaries of the group. Judaism provided straightforward answers to the question, 'Who is in, who is out?' These answers were, in principle, matters of fact that could be checked and established beyond doubt. Jesus, however, could be quoted as one who rejected this style of thinking: he would not endorse John's attempt to stop a man who exorcized demons using the name of Jesus but refused to be a member of the group of disciples (Mark 9:38–41). There was a parable (in Matthew 25:31–46) in which those who are blessed and those who are not are equally surprised when they are given their verdicts at the last judgment.

'Who has faith?' is a notoriously difficult question to answer. Fortunately, we do not need to know. We are not to judge; we must leave that to the only one who can!

PRAYER

Thank you for making us the descendants of Abraham, by faith.
Thank you for the promise of our blessing.
Thank you that this promise is for everybody.

15

Curse or blessing?
Law or faith?

In these five verses, Paul quotes four passages from scripture: in verse 10, from Deuteronomy 27:26; in verse 11 from Habakkuk 2:4; in verse 12, from Leviticus 18:5; and in verse 13, from Deuteronomy 27:26. He wants to demonstrate from scripture that being right with God depends on faith, not on keeping the Law of Moses. On the contrary, keeping the Law puts one under God's curse. Christ came to deliver us from this curse, by being crucified for us; his purpose was that we might receive what was promised to Abraham, the blessing of God which is the gift of the Holy Spirit (thus tying this paragraph into the argument about receiving the Spirit, in 3:1–5).

As we have seen already (in the Introduction) the letter to the Galatians is rich in contrasts. Pairs of opposites are lined up against one another. Here, Paul contrasts 'curse' with 'blessing', observing and obeying 'the works of the law' with 'faith'. The mistake of the Galatians, he believes, is to try to join the wrong side. They are turning away from a life of blessing to adopt one that he can only describe as cursed.

It needs to be said that this was not how Judaism appeared to the majority of those who had been brought up as Jews from birth; nor how it appeared to the Galatians who were thinking of living as Jews. The Law was compared to light for those in darkness and water for the thirsty; it was a delight to study it and it rejoiced the heart to keep it. The author of Psalm 119 composed twenty-two eight line stanzas, acrostics on the Hebrew alphabet, in celebration of the Law. Paul's argument is, therefore, not that the Galatians will be unhappy if they keep the Law but that they will not be within the blessing of God. They may enjoy keeping the regulations of Judaism, but they will no longer be free and they will no longer receive the Spirit. They will, he says, be 'cut off from Christ' (5:4).

Paul's arguments may strike us as excessive, oratorical rather than balanced and carefully nuanced. He is writing to Gentiles and he is dealing with a practical question: should they do what the new teachers in Galatia are telling them to do, or not? If he is not using a sledge-hammer to crack a nut, he is certainly drawing on all his resources of scriptural knowledge to defeat his opponents on their own ground.

To understand Paul's conviction that what he is saying is what God means him to say, we need to understand that the source of his certainty lies in his sense of gratitude to Christ: 'he loved me', and not only that; he 'gave himself for me', to death; to becoming a 'curse for us' by the manner of his execution—'Cursed is everyone who hangs on a tree'.

Paul, the Galatians to whom he writes, and we who read his letter, can see something that had not been at all clear before the crucifixion and resurrection of Jesus. We can see that God does not deal with us on the basis of rules and procedures laid down in books and tradition, some of which must appear (at least to us) as arbitrary and irrational. Instead, God relates to us in ways that are personal: the words that are used are words that describe interpersonal relationships: faith, love, gratitude, goodwill, peace and so on.

PRAYER

Thank you for treating us as adult persons.
Stop us from regressing into infantile attitudes.
Give us the boldness that must accompany faith.

Promise, not Law

Paul continues to build up the list of contrasted words in order to persuade the Galatians that if they do what they seem set to do they will be making a serious mistake. He begins with the point that when a will is made it cannot be changed by subsequent events. In Greek, as also in Hebrew, one word could mean both a will and a covenant. What Paul wants to make clear is that the Law was given to Israel only at the time of the exodus from Egypt, 430 years after the patriarchs. (He draws this information from Exodus 12:40: 'The time that the Israelites had lived in Egypt was four hundred and thirty years'.)

When God was dealing with the patriarchs he dealt in promises. When he gave Israel the Law through Moses he dealt in commandments that had to be obeyed. The latter cannot abolish the former: wills cannot be altered. Therefore God deals with us through promises, not through the Law.

A difficulty could be raised. If we are arguing about circumcision, then it could be said that it was required of Abraham in Genesis 17. Circumcision was there before the time of Moses. Someone may have pointed this out to Paul, or he may have noticed the difficulty for himself, because when he writes to the Romans he adjusts the argument to take account of it and makes the same point by saying that God made promises to Abraham before Abraham was circumcised (Romans 4:9-12). Faith preceded circumcision. Abraham is the father of all who believe, whether they are circumcised or not.

There is another deduction that Paul makes from the quotation in this paragraph from Genesis 13:15: 'and to your offspring' (literally, 'seed'). It is a singular word and so, he says, it refers 'to one person, Christ'. It might be objected that 'offspring' or 'seed' is a collective noun, referring to a group, and that its being in the singular signifies nothing more than that Abraham's descendants can be classed as one group. No doubt Paul would regard this as a quibble. He saw meaning in the singular word and found it providential. We do not know whether his readers found it so too, but (for what it is worth) he does not (so far as we know) seem to have used the argument again.

The point of real substance in this paragraph is the contrast between promise and Law. Law introduces a condition into an arrangement. The one who gives the law is saying 'You must do this; and if you do not then the arrangement is dissolved and you have no further claims on me.' A publisher's agreement with an author, for example, states what the author must do: the requirements and conditions. If they are not kept the publisher is released from his side of the arrangement. But promises are promises. They stand—whatever the other party may or may not do. They are unconditional, unilateral and indissoluble.

In the case in point, God was promising to give the land of Canaan to Abraham and to his offspring (Genesis 13:15). There were no 'ifs'—'If you do this, I shall give you the land'. It was an absolute statement of what God would do. Therefore, since God could not contradict himself, he must do it.

When Paul uses the word 'inheritance' (3:18) he is using the term that was frequently applied to the land of Canaan in scripture (in the Greek translation). But to Paul the meaning of the inheritance is now to be found not in the literal sense but in the metaphorical. It refers, he believes, to the gift of the Spirit and to the life of the age to come, of which the gift of the Spirit is the first instalment. Paul is, in fact, repeating in another way the ideas which he had expressed at the beginning of chapter 3: 'Did you receive the Spirit by doing the works of the law or by believing what you heard?' The Spirit was given to us without our doing anything: it just happened out of the blue.

We can see here why Paul thought that the gospel was good news. It was something for nothing, like treasure found in a field, or an unexpectedly valuable pearl that could be sold for a huge profit. (Matthew 13:44–46). God does not hedge his goodness with qualifications: he is sheer generosity.

PRAYER
Thank you for your promise.
Thank you for your bounty.
Thank you for your gifts.

17
No turning back

Paul thinks of the members of the churches he has founded as his children. The gospel was the means by which he caused them to be born and he is both mother and father to them. (He will use the metaphor in this letter at 4:19). What he is doing now is weaning them off their desire to keep the Law; and the method that he adopts here is to find reasons for the Law that they can see are no longer valid.

'Why then the Law?' is the question anyone hearing the letter might raise at this point. Why did God give it to Israel if it was not to be kept? Nothing in scripture said the Law's validity was only for a time. Circumcision, for example, was said to be for all generations. It was an everlasting covenant (Genesis 17:9–14). It was God's will, and God does not change his mind. This is Paul's problem: how can he persuade the Galatians to do this most unscriptural thing—turn away from their desire (surely, they would say, a good, God-given desire) to obey God's will as it was set out by God in the five books of the Law?

The first thing he says is that the Law 'was added'; it was not part of God's original promise to Abraham. Nothing added later can remove the force of the promise, as he just said (3:15). The inferiority of the Law is manifest in the delay before it was given. Why was it added? 'Because of transgressions'. The meaning may be: to create transgressions. The REB translates it as: 'To make wrongdoing a legal offence'. Without the Law we might do things but not know that they were wrong. Of many things we might say: 'They are natural; we all do them; what is wrong with that?' Jealousy, envy, lust, selfishness, greed and anger are all so common that if no one said they were sinful we might not know. Paul is emphasizing the negative aspect of the Law: it can show you that you are wrong and that you do wrong things.

He says next that the Law was always intended to be temporary: 'until the offspring would come to whom the promise had been made'. He is building on the passage from Genesis that he had referred to (v. 16): 'And to your offspring'. That referred to Christ, he had said. Now he draws the conclusion that, because the promise was to Abraham and Christ, the Law (added later than the promise) ends when the promise is fulfilled. God meant the Law to be temporary;

that is Paul's belief. To keep it is to observe instructions that are out of date. The Law has, if you may put it this way, passed its sell-by-date.

There is more to come: 'It was ordained through angels'. Jews believed that there were angels present when God gave the Law to Moses at Sinai; but no Jew had previously said (so far as we know) that the angels ordained, or promulgated, the Law. Scripture had said that it was written by the finger of God, and this left little room for the activity of angels. Paul is therefore going beyond what any rabbi would have said about the Law. Angels were inferior to God, and therefore the mediation of angels in the giving of the Law made it a less perfect expression of God's will than it would have been if the revelation had been direct.

Finally, Paul says, the giving of the Law involved the activity of a 'mediator'—i.e. Moses. This again, he believes, shows the inferiority of the Law to the promise. The fact of the presence of a mediator between God, the angels and Israel, explains why it is that the Law is no longer in force. God acted alone when he made promises. There were too many others involved in the promulgation of the Law, and it suffered from their association with it.

These are extraordinary things for a first-century Jew, who had been a Pharisee, to say about the core of his former beliefs. There is no scripture for him to quote in this paragraph. He depends here not on something that was in scripture: but on what God has done in calling him to be an apostle—and in the conflicts and tensions of Paul's life, in his arguing with apostles in Jerusalem and Antioch, and in protecting his children from the errors of the trouble-makers.

We can gauge the force of the impact these events had on Paul by the lengths to which he is going here. He is turning his back on what he had believed to be God's greatest gift and man's dearest joy in order to embrace something else: a different way of relating to God.

Instead of laws, promises. Instead of books, a person. Instead of limits and restrictions, freedom. It was like coming out of prison, coming of age, being given the front door key, opening your own bank account, passing the driving test, getting your first car.

PRAYER

Show us what you have given us.
Let us not revert to childishness.
Push us out of the nest.

18 Release from prison

What is the relationship between the Law and God's promises? It is not hostile to them, Paul says. (This seems to be the meaning of the Greek which is translated 'contradict' in the NRSV.) The Law no more opposes God's promises than the prison service opposes the liberty of the citizen. It keeps people away from liberty temporarily but it does not threaten it.

Paul speculates that God could have given us a law that would have given us access to freedom and life had he wished to do so; but the fact is, he has not. He has given us a law that acts like a gaoler and keeps us locked up.

One way to think of this is to realize that what the Law of the Jews did was to create divisions into what was commanded and what was prohibited. There were working days and non-working days; clean food and unclean food; Jews and Gentiles; what was appropriate for men and what was appropriate for women. There were also those who kept the Law and those who didn't.

Such divisions are just what sin delights in. They create situations in which all sorts of selfish and destructive tendencies can come into play. 'The scripture has imprisoned all things under the power of sin': it has increased the scope we have for sinning by setting up false aims and intentions.

If the Law divides, then what God does is to unite. He is one, as Paul has just said (3:20), and he brings things into unity with himself so that divisions will be overcome. 'Faith in Jesus Christ' gives us access to a way of living that abolishes the differences in which sin flourishes. This is 'the inheritance' of which Paul has spoken (3:18), the Promised Land now made available and accessible to believers. Here competition, rivalry, selfishness, strife, hatred and jealousy are overcome.

We can see what Paul was expecting to happen from another letter he wrote, probably soon after this one. Christ would come from heaven and destroy 'every ruler and every authority and power'. He would reign until he had 'put all his enemies under his feet'. Then he would hand over rulership to God the Father, and in this way God would be all in all (1 Corinthians 15:23–28).

The angelic beings (rulers, authorities and powers) that had to be destroyed were responsible for the divisions of the world into nations and classes, and for all mutual opposition and hatred between human groups and individuals. The Law was one of these powers: 'The power of sin is the law' (1 Corinthians 15:56). 'The law came in, with the result that the trespass multiplied' (Romans 5:20). Sin, trespass, law and death must all be abolished before God can be everything to everything, uniting his whole creation to himself in peace and harmony.

PRAYER

Thank you for ending the term of our imprisonment.
Thank you for bringing us into the new world.
Thank you for abolishing all that we feared.

19
No more divisions

Paul now introduces a way of thinking about God's dealings with the world which was unusual at that time but which was to have many applications in the future. He sees past history as made up of periods of time in which God acted in different ways.

There was the time when God made promises and people lived by faith—in the age of the patriarchs, Abraham, Isaac and Jacob. There was the time when God gave Israel the Law through Moses. There was the time when the offspring of Abraham—Christ—came: and Christ was the end of the Law and the beginning of a new age of faith. When Paul says here, 'Before faith came' and 'Until faith would be revealed', he is abbreviating a larger expression: 'Before Christ came to begin the era of faith'.

The second period, from Moses to Jesus, was a time of imprisonment and loss of liberty. The Law confined us, and would not allow us to do certain things. It was, Paul says, 'our disciplinarian'. He uses a word that means, literally, 'child-leader' and was used of slaves who took children to school. In Paul's time such people were not held in respect.

That is all now over: Christ has come; faith has come; we are living in a new age, and the disciplinarian's time is over. We can see for ourselves that this is so. It is obvious that God no longer recognizes the distinction between Jews and Gentiles, which the Law had created by means of circumcision. Faith is what counts, now; and faith is non-discriminatory, non-exclusive. All sorts of people believe. All sorts of people have received the Spirit—the Gentile Galatians for example.

The NRSV translation here (v. 27), 'As many of you as were baptized', is unfortunate. It might suggest that baptism among Christians took the place that circumcision had had among the Jews and thus provided a new way of dividing people—the baptized and the unbaptized. Paul's intention is to say the opposite: baptism abolishes divisions, it does not create them. Baptism is putting on Christ—being dressed so as to be seen as him. He ate and drank with tax collectors and sinners; he died for everybody, and everybody died when he died. A baptized person cannot distinguish between different classes or divisions in society: distinguishing is abolished.

The most relevant division for the Galatians was that between 'Jews' and the rest of humanity ('Greeks'). The Galatians thought that this was still a valid distinction but Paul does not. 'Slave' and 'free' was also an obvious distinction in a society that depended on slavery for its functioning. In the Christian congregation, however, you could not tell who was which: the Spirit did not observe society's rules. 'Male' and 'female', Paul says, is a third distinction that has been abolished. In their relationship with Christ they are equal; and each of them is an equally important member of the body of Christ. (Paul himself found it difficult to put the second and third of these abolitions into practice—neither slave nor free, male nor female—and so have his successors.)

Christ has done for everybody the one thing that needed to be done: he has died for everyone. Every individual, Jew or Greek, slave or free, male or female, is the person for whom Christ died. One label can be attached to every human being.

PRAYER

Let me make no distinctions.
Let me write no one off.
Let me not give honour to one more than to others.

20 No longer children

Paul makes over again the point he had been arguing in the previous paragraph. (He seems to attribute less intelligence to the foolish Galatians than he will to the Romans when the time comes to write to them.)

To start now to keep the Mosaic Law is to do something that is out of date. The heir of a property, the future owner, is not able to exercise his ownership until he comes of age. Until then he has no more power or control over it than a slave has. He is under the control of others until he inherits.

Similarly, Jews and Gentiles were both dealt with by God through restrictions and limitations. The Jews were controlled by the Law, the Gentiles by spiritual beings—some class of angels, referred to here as 'the elemental spirits of the world'.

But now that Christ has come God is dealing with us as adult, mature, grown up people. God's Son came as one who was under the Law (he lived as a Jew), and this was not to be as an example for us to follow him (as the trouble-makers may have said) but to set us free from the Law.

The NRSV translation has caused disastrous confusion in this passage by attempting to be politically correct and changing 'sons' to 'children' (vv. 5–6) and 'son' to 'child' (v. 7). Paul's point is the complete opposite of what the NRSV says. He means, 'You no are no longer children'; you are adult, come of age, you have inherited. 'The date set by the father' has come.

How do we know this? Once again Paul employs the argument from the facts. These Galatian Christians, to whom Paul is writing in Greek, sometimes speak in Aramaic, the language of Jesus and his followers. They say *Abba*! They address God as 'Father!' There was a time when they would not have done so—before Paul came to Galatia. It was Paul, the gospel, Jesus and the Spirit that made the difference. These were the markers that the age of the Law was over and the time of the inheritance had come. They were adults now, not children.

The fact that some of the Galatians wanted to keep the Law, and that Paul had to write this angry letter to dissuade them, shows how attractive a religion that provides plenty of regulations for behaviour can be to some people. They wanted to keep the festivals of the Jews (4:10); they would have followed Peter's example at Antioch and kept food laws (2:11–12); the males in the congregation were thinking of the possibility of circumcision (5:2). Paul thinks this willingness to hand oneself over to the observances of religious practices is a sign of weakness, fear and absence of faith. It is a going back to childish ways, not what God requires of them.

Because something is religious it is not necessarily good. There is such a thing as bad religion. The test (which this passage suggests) is: 'Are we being dealt with as adults?' To do things for which no reasonable case can be made (e.g. circumcision and the food laws), or to try to believe impossible things, is not compatible with God's methods of dealing with us. He deals with humans through a human being. His Spirit enlightens our minds. We are made to think.

PRAYER
Stop me from being unreasonable.
Help me to think.
Inspire my mind.

21 Not back into slavery

The Galatians to whom Paul is writing had been Gentiles; otherwise the question of circumcision would never have arisen. As Gentiles they had worshipped pagan gods which, Paul points out, are not gods at all. He thought of them as some sort of malicious spiritual beings, like fallen angels or demons. Therefore, before Paul preached in Galatia and before the Galatians believed the gospel, they 'did not know God'.

The result of his preaching was the opposite to the situation before he came; instead of not knowing God, they came 'to know God'. Paul says that, but then immediately withdraws it. The truth is not simply the reverse of the previous state of affairs. The change from before to after was not the result of something the Galatians did. It was not a human act that altered the situation. The revelation of God's Son, to Paul (1:16) and to the Galatians (as he will explain in the next paragraph, 4:12–20), was the action of God. Paul therefore withdraws: 'you have come to know God', and replaces it with: 'to be known by God'. 'How God thinks of us is not only more important, but infinitely more important' than how we think of him (C.S. Lewis, *Screwtape Proposes a Toast*, Fount, 1965, page 103).

'To be known by God' means more than his awareness of us or his having information about us. It involves his attitude towards us, his intention and purpose for us. The whole story of the exodus of the Israelites from Egypt is preceded by the statement, 'God looked upon the Israelites, and God took notice of them' (Exodus 2:25). God's knowledge of the Galatians is the cause of both Paul's mission to Galatia and the faith of the Galatians that followed. It is God's decision to be for us and to rescue us from destruction and to associate himself with us. This is how it was in the exodus and this is how it is with those to whom the gospel is preached.

It makes the Galatians' desire to keep the Law all the more tragic: 'How can you turn back again to the weak and beggarly elemental spirits?'—that is, the 'no gods' that had held them in subjection before faith came. How can you turn to them from the God who turned to you? But this is what they are doing. The trouble-makers have introduced them to the observance of a religious calendar and they have accepted this. Paul thinks it is the thin edge of a wedge: they will become observant Jews in no time.

The whole of Paul's ministry in Galatia will be wasted if this happens. He regards joining the synagogue as on the same level as being a pagan. In both cases freedom was restricted by rules, distinctions were established between what was lawful and what was not, and there was nothing to show that the Spirit was present. It was all superstitions, taboos and irrational traditions.

To us in the late twentieth century this must seem un-ecumenical and hidebound, unappreciative of the deep insights of Judaism, which was the religion of Jesus. Paul saw it differently. He was convinced that the gospel had given him an altogether new insight into God and into how God wanted him to live. God's knowledge of Paul created a new situation for Paul. It involved him in a life of activity that he would never have embarked upon had it not been for God. He was sure that to call God 'Father!' was something new and revolutionary.

PRAYER

Thank you for your knowledge of us.
Do not let what you have done for us be wasted.
Keep us from falling back into slavery.

22 Remember what happened

The meaning of the opening sentences of this paragraph is obscure: 'Become as I am, for I also have become as you are'. Literally translated, the Greek says simply: 'Become as I because I also as you'. Paul is about to remind them of his preaching to them in Galatia when they first believed. At that time he had already abandoned the strict keeping of the Law in which he had been brought up. He wants the Galatians to do the same: give up both their pagan past and their Law-keeping future, into which the trouble-makers are trying to seduce them.

'You have done me no wrong' refers to what happened at the time of his initial visit, as he goes on to say. He is once again recalling facts—facts now that were well within their own experience and can be recalled 'as if it were only yesterday'. The extraordinary thing about that first visit was that the faith of the Galatians happened exactly when it was least expected. It was a miracle.

Paul was a sick man; that was the only reason why he had stopped in Galatia and not gone on more quickly to preach elsewhere. (We do not know what his illness was, and there is no need for us to do so.) Sickness, like any other unfortunate circumstance, would be interpreted by the Galatians as evidence that Paul was not sent by God. God's messengers, they would assume, would be protected by the power of their God, and be immune to sickness, accidents, dangers and disasters of every kind. (We know that the Corinthians believed this; that is why Paul refutes it in 2 Corinthians. It would seem extraordinary to any first century pagan or Jew that God's servants could be strong when they were weak.)

So the temptation to which the Galatians were exposed by Paul's illness was to write off Paul, and Paul's supposed God, as ineffectual and useless. But they did not; that was what was so extraordinary. The miracle was that they welcomed Paul as an angel (or messenger; it is the same word in Greek) of God. They knew that God had blessed them. ('What has become of the good will you felt?' is literally 'where then is the blessedness?' and expects the answer, 'nowhere'. They have forgotten that God gave them faith. They have forgotten all that he has ever done for them.)

At the time of Paul's first visit to Galatia they had been so deeply aware of their debt to God and to Paul his messenger that they would have given him their eyes—and they could scarcely have given him anything more valuable. But now they think of Paul in a very different way. They have gone over to the side of his opponents and he has become their enemy. He has done this simply by telling them the truth: reminding them of the gospel he had preached, of the faith God had given them, of the Spirit they had received, and of the miracles God had performed.

Paul's way of dealing with the Galatian problem may seem to us rabbinical and quaint: the quotation of texts, often out of context; allegorical interpretations of scripture, and so on. But in fact he is never far from rubbing their noses in indisputable happenings. His life really had changed—from persecutor to apostle. The churches in Judea really had known this—and confirmed it. The Galatians really had received the Spirit through faith—and not through keeping the Law. Paul really had been a sick man, no advertisement for a God to be believed in by first-century pagans. All they had been given to see was a crucified Christ present in his sick apostle—but they really had been blessed with faith.

Telling the truth can make you an enemy of those to whom you do it. Jesus said, 'The truth will make you free'; but they put him to death for saying it.

PRAYER

We fear the truth and resist it.
We do not want to remember your goodness.
Forgive our perversity.

23 Paul is their father and their mother

Paul was not writing this letter to us. He was not writing it for anyone other than the Christian congregation in Galatia in the middle of the first century AD. He could assume that they knew things about which we are largely ignorant. When he says: 'They make much of you' he is, it seems, referring to the trouble-makers in Galatia—and his readers knew exactly what he meant and what they were doing.

His opponents were zealous in the attention they paid to the congregations, but Paul says that it is not genuine love. Their motives are false. Paul's opponents are telling the Galatians that they are not proper members of Abraham's family, so that the Galatians will ask them to show them what they must do. (The answer they will receive will be, 'Keep the law, just as all Abraham's genuine children do.') Genuine love is good, but they will not get this from the trouble-makers. The only one who really loves them is Paul—and, he implies, no one else.

He was the first to preach the gospel in Galatia. That gave him a relationship with them that no one else could have. He describes this relationship, in another letter, as begetting, fathering: 'For though you might have ten thousand guardians in Christ, you do not have many fathers. Indeed in Christ Jesus I became your father through the gospel' (1 Corinthians 4:15). In this metaphysical sense he calls them 'my little children'.

But then he switches the metaphor: he is their mother, in the process of 'childbirth' all over 'again until Christ is formed' in them. He has both the responsibility of the father for starting the family and the pain of the mother in bringing them to birth. It does not matter if the metaphor is mixed. All that matters is that he tells them of his love for them and of the pain that they are causing him—and that he uses the fact that they are his converts to drive a wedge between them and the trouble-makers.

Paul tells the Romans that he made it his ambition to proclaim the good news, not where Christ had already been named, so that he did not build on someone else's foundation (Romans 15:20). He says this with the implied criticism of those who do not keep such a rule; they poach his converts, but he never does that to them.

If we are right in thinking that his opponents in Galatia are part of a larger movement, centred in Jerusalem, which we also meet in Paul's letters to the Romans, the Corinthians and the Philippians, then we can see that they seem to have adopted a policy of travelling round behind Paul, making up the deficiencies in his ministry (as they believed). Paul's irritation and anger are understandable.

To us, Paul may seem over-possessive. We might say, 'It does not matter if they want to do things that I personally do not approve of. And if they find other preachers more helpful than I, let them listen to them. It is all one God, one Christ, one Holy Spirit, whoever preaches and teaches'.

Paul certainly did not take this view of the matter. He did not think that it was unimportant what you believed, or that it did not matter what religious practices you observed. He took the matter very seriously: 'Listen! I, Paul, am telling you that if you let yourselves be circumcised, Christ will be of no benefit to you' (5:2). Their salvation hung in the balance. He must stop them from making a mistake that would cost them their eternal life.

PRAYER

Give us genuine love for one another.
Make us care for others
Help us to be serious.

24 The two branches of Abraham's family

Paul now uses the scriptural account of Abraham's descendants to demonstrate to his reader in Galatia that, according to the Law itself, it would be wrong for them to keep the Law. It seems highly likely that his opponents were saying: 'Unless you are circumcised you are not part of Abraham's family, that is, the people of God'. Paul is replying: 'By reading Genesis in a certain way we can see that freedom from the Law was foretold in the Law.' It is Paul's final argument against his opponents, and to them (though not perhaps to us) it may have seemed devastating, destroying their whole case.

We have seen already that in this letter Paul is forcing the issue into a choice between alternatives and that he defines the alternatives by means of opposites. He is saying: 'Here is one way, and there is the only other way; choose which you will go along. One is Spirit; the other, flesh. One is gospel; the other, Law. One is blessing; the other, curse.' He now finds these alternatives in the patriarchal legends, symbolized by Abraham's two sons.

The names of the two sons are Ishmael and Isaac. Ishmael, who was born before Isaac, was the son of Abraham by Hagar, the slave of Sarah, Abraham's wife; Isaac was the son of Sarah, conceived when both she and Abraham were of great age. (The name Isaac means 'he laughs': see Genesis 17:19 and 18:9–15.) There was nothing in any way remarkable about the conception and birth of Ishmael; it happened just like any other birth; Paul says it was 'according to the flesh' (v. 23). Isaac's birth was totally unexpected, because of the age of his parents (Paul will make this point more explicitly in Romans 4:19) and Sarah's record of infertility. Isaac was therefore 'born through the promise'. God had said it would happen, and that was why it did happen (Genesis 17:15–22). Each son is the ancestor of a nation: Ishmael of the Arabs and Isaac of the Hebrews.

Paul, however, interprets the two branches of Abraham's family allegorically, taking as his key to this exposition the status of the two mothers (Sarah was a *free woman*, Hagar was a *slave woman*) and bringing in also the contrast between *the promise* and *the flesh*. In this way Sarah and Isaac are the symbols those who believe in Christ while Hagar and Ishmael are the symbols of those who do not. Thus freedom (from the Law) is the mark of believers, slavery to the Law is the mark of unbelievers.

Paul also contrasts Mount Sinai and Jerusalem with the Jerusalem in heaven; the former are associated with Law and the latter with freedom. Finally, he brings in a quotation from Isaiah (54:1) where a childless person (here he means Sarah) is promised more children than a married woman (i.e. Hagar): believers will outnumber unbelievers.

Paul did not find this interpretation of the two women and their sons in scripture: he read it in, rather than reading it out. He read scripture in the light of his Christian experience. And the lesson he learned here was that Abraham's family are not to keep the Law, because they are free. The Law tells us not to keep the Law. It is a *tour de force*.

PRAYER

Show us the extent of our freedom.
Help us to believe in the Spirit.
Thank you for the church, our mother.

Christian liberty

Paul now applies the allegory to the situation in Galatia. Those who believe in Christ are 'children of the promise, like Isaac'. He does not mean anything similar to our expression 'promising children'—people with talent, high IQs, future leaders, etc. 'Children of the promise' means people who have come into existence through a special act of God and not in the usual, normal way. They are exceptions because they are believers: and faith requires a gift from God—the gift of being a believer.

The background to the expression, which is essential for understanding its meaning, is Genesis 17:15ff.: God's promise was the cause of Sarah's conception. God's gift of faith was the cause of the Galatians' believing. (We are to remember that they had every reason not to believe Paul, but to 'scorn' and 'despise' him, 4:14.)

Paul then quotes Genesis again: this time it is Genesis 21:10, in which Abraham was told by Sarah to expel Hagar and Ishmael; the inheritance was not to be shared between the slave-branch and the free-branch of the family. Jews persecute the followers of Christ now, Paul is saying, just as Ishmael persecuted Isaac then. The future for the family of Abraham lay with Isaac—those who were free—and that is how it was. Do not therefore attempt to join the wrong side.

'Christ has set us free' by his death and resurrection. He has died the kind of death that the Law declared to be cursed (3:13). He accepted the position of being condemned and executed, and the result is that the whole system of Jewish Law under which he was judged has been brought to an end.

Notice once more the word 'again' in 5:1. The 'yoke of slavery' is the Law of Moses, but the people Paul is writing to had been Gentiles before they believed. To be circumcised now, and to keep the Law, will be to go back 'again' to where they were before they believed. There is no distinction in this respect between Judaism and paganism; both are described here as 'slavery'.

Paul recognizes coming into faith as a kind of living that is new, different, and totally strange. He will list some of the aspects of it in the next chapter, but notice in particular *joy* and *peace*. Anyone who

has experienced these knows that they are extraordinary and unbelievable—so extraordinary and unbelievable that they could easily be
dismissed and lost in a return to everyday normal existence. Paul
will say, in another letter, that 'the peace of God surpasses all understanding' (Philippians 4:7). Our hold on it is tenuous; we must 'stand
firm' and not let trouble-makers try to convince us that we do not
have it.

The irony was that it was religious trouble-makers who were causing the trouble and causing one sort of religion to destroy another.

PRAYER

Thank you for freedom, joy and peace.
Help us to resist pressure to doubt it.
No submission to fear!

26
Either–or

Paul believes it is not a matter of indifference whether the Galatians keep the Law, or whether they do not. Nor is it possible to pick and choose. It is either–or—and it is: all or nothing.

It is either–or, as he has argued all the way through the letter. The two ways are alternatives: you cannot go in two directions at the same time. There is salvation through Christ on the one hand, and there is circumcision and the other laws on the other hand. The Galatians must choose. There had been a before and after in the life of Paul: persecution before, proclamation after. No compromise was possible: 'if you let yourselves be circumcised, Christ will be of no benefit to you'.

It is also all or nothing. Circumcision introduces them to a life of obedience to the Law, and this may involve more than they had expected: its detailed instructions covered the whole of life. Paul then says it again: Christ and the Law are incompatible as ways of salvation.

Paul says nothing about the historical reasons for the crucifixion, or on what charge Jesus was condemned, or even whether he was condemned by a Jewish court. He may not have known. What he did know was that he had thought that the followers of Jesus should be eliminated and he had sought to do so. In his own experience, Christ and the Law had been opposite: enemies, mutually exclusive, and this had ended in the crucifixion of Jesus and the conflict between the authorities of Judaism and the early church.

Perhaps there was another element too. Those who kept the Law within the church at Jerusalem may have been (or been thought to be) the instigators of the trouble in Galatia and indeed wherever Paul had established any congregations. The conflict was a daily problem, and he could not dismiss it as of no importance. He refers to it as danger from false brothers and sisters (2 Corinthians 11:26).

Paul will now move on from this subject to another and the rest of the letter will be dominated by two main ideas. First, we do not need the Law because we are led by the Spirit. Secondly, we do not need the Law because there is one commandment that sums it all up: *You shall love your neighbour as yourself.*

We live in a transition period, praying for the end of this age to come quickly. That is the righteousness we are looking forward to, when God will declare us his sons and daughters (Matthew 5:9). Distinctions made by the Law (Jew and Gentile, etc.) are now matters of the past. The evidence is there in the congregations: they are meetings of believers, and they are held together by love: 'the only thing that counts is faith working through love'.

PRAYER

Thank you for the simplicity of the gospel.
Thank you for the abolition of false religion.
Thank you for the clarity of the alternatives.

27 The offence of the cross

The Galatians have changed course since they began to believe. Something had happened in Paul's absence that had made them adopt new ideas to which Paul violently objects. We know only from what we can gather from Paul's letter who it was and what was said, and this is not much.

Paul uses a metaphor from the games (as he does again in 1 Corinthians 9:24–27). They were 'running well', but someone interfered with them (the literal meaning of the Greek word would be 'cut in') and stopped them from 'obeying the truth', that is, the gospel as he had preached it to them. They knew what he was talking about, and he does not go on to identify the intruder. What he does do is say that this influence had not come from God (i.e. the one who had called them to believe; see 1:6). It must, therefore, be of the devil; there was no third possibility in a situation such as this. He then switches to another metaphor, this time bread-making. You do not need much 'yeast' to 'leaven the whole batch' (compare Matthew 13:33; and 1 Corinthians 5:6ff. where leaven is used to refer to something evil that must be removed; incest in 1 Corinthians, false teaching in Galatians).

Paul believes that the Galatians will do what he is telling them to do. We do not know exactly what happened next, but it may be that the preservation of the letter points to their having taken his advice and rejected the trouble-makers.

'Whoever it is that is confusing you' (compare 1:7, 'there are some who are confusing you'; there it is in the plural, 'some'; here it is in the singular, 'whoever') 'will pay the penalty' or, as in the REB, 'must bear God's judgment'. Does the 'whoever it is' mean, whatever his position and status? Even if he is the leader of the church in Jerusalem? Even if he is the Lord's brother?

Then, once again, the argument from observable facts is brought in. It cannot be, as some say, that Paul still preaches circumcision. If he were, he would not be being persecuted by Jews or by Jewish Christians. The undeniable fact that people are against Paul shows that he is still saying things that make them angry with him.

What he preaches is 'the cross': that Jesus, God's Son, was put to death by crucifixion, and that this was according to the scriptures and for our sins (1 Corinthians 15:3). Christ has taken the place of the Law. Those who have received the Spirit are those who believe in him, not those who keep the Law. The saving moment is identified as an act of suffering and shame. This is why Paul speaks of it as an 'offence' (the word is *skandalon*), something that causes you to trip and fall over. This is what the gospel is to Jews; they 'demand signs' (i.e. miracles) but to be crucified is no miracle at all (1 Corinthians 1:22–25).

The anger of Paul with those who are causing trouble in Galatia is evident in the next verse, which one commentator describes as 'downright rude and even objectionable' (Ziesler, *The Epistle to the Galatians*, page 73).

PRAYER

Let us not forget how offensive faith is.
Let us not be surprised that people find it so, and find us so.
Help me to believe that truth will prevail.

28

Only one commandment

A new section of the letter begins at this point and continues to 6:10. The theme now is *love* and *Spirit*. It may be that Paul's opponents were saying, 'If we do not retain the Law of Moses there will be nothing to prevent us from falling into anarchy. We need the Law to stop us from following our own unbridled selfishness.' It may be that; or it may be that Paul anticipated such an argument. Whichever it was, he now takes up the subject, showing that there are other resources available: *love*, and God's *Spirit*.

'You were called', by God. Paul has used the word three times already in this letter (1:6, 15; 5:8) and in each case of God calling people to believe. The fact of their believing is due entirely to God, not to themselves. He chose them, predestined them, sent Paul to preach to them, gave them the Spirit. Their faith is not of their own doing, but of God's; so who are they to change the terms which were laid down from the beginning? These terms didn't include keeping the Law.

On the contrary, they were invited by God to be free—both from the fears and restraints imposed by their pagan religion and from any other kinds of limitation (such as the Law of Moses). Paul has already contrasted Law and freedom (e.g. in 4:21—5:1, the allegory of the two women, one free and the other a slave). By 'freedom', here, therefore, he means exception from the Law which imposed prohibitions on its observers.

Nevertheless, freedom does not mean freedom to sin. Nor does it mean that if we were free we would have nothing to keep us from sinning. It would be a misunderstanding of freedom, and a misuse of it, to treat it as a bridgehead from which self-indulgence could advance. (The word which Paul uses, *sarx*, translated 'the flesh', is an expression that refers to all kinds of self-centredness and not only what are sometimes called 'sins of the flesh'.)

Paul is not afraid of paradoxes. He knows that the gospel can only be expressed by using them: glory/shame; power/weakness;

wisdom/foolishness, and so on. He produces them now to explain what the new life is: To be free is to be the slave of others; this is the effect of love (Greek: *agape*): Christ's love made him our slave, dying for us; our love for one another makes us the slaves of each other.

This is, after all, what the Law itself commanded (Leviticus 19:18): 'You shall love your neighbour as yourself'; and that one commandment sums up all that God intends us to do and all that the Law was intended to achieve. Of course God does not mean us to use our freedom in a destructive way; but we only need one controlling aim to keep us from that.

We shall have more scope for love if we detach it from the Law of Moses. As long as it is part of Moses' Law it may have to be qualified: 'Who is my neighbour?' (Luke 10:29). But taken without any possible restrictions (that neighbour means fellow-Israelite, etc.), love can be exercised without discrimination: it was while we were his enemies that 'we were reconciled to God through the death of his Son' (Romans 5:10).

PRAYER

Thank you for our calling.
Thank you for our freedom.
Teach us to fulfil your only commandment.

GALATIANS 5:16-18
The hard road

Paul is not starry-eyed about the Christian life and he does not want his readers to dismiss him as impractical. He knows how members of Christian communities can 'bite and devour' one another; he had a long-running case in Corinth which was probably still on at the time of the writing of Galatians.

The Galatians had received the Spirit (3:2); there could be no denying that. But to have received the Spirit was not the end of the problem. They must still be exhorted to 'live by the Spirit'. The word that Paul uses literally means 'walk'. God's commandments are a way, or road, or path. To obey them is to walk or run in his way. To disobey the commandments of God is to step off his path, to trespass.

The believer is aware of two things, not of only one, in this respect. There is both the power and insight given by the Spirit, but there are also 'the desires of the flesh'. He means, as we have seen, self-centredness and its accompanying destructiveness of others. Or to put it more bluntly: we can either love on another, or not; but if we do not love one another, we shall destroy one another.

We are thus prevented from doing what we want: we are the scene of conflict and warfare: *Spirit* against *flesh* and *flesh* against *Spirit*.

What we must do is choose *Spirit*, and say no to *flesh*. There is one who will lead us: a guide who will come with us along the road. It is the Spirit; you can be *led by the Spirit*.

Talk of two ways, of walking and trespassing, is all found in the scriptures we call the Old Testament. But there, it is the Law that provides the way of God's commandments and is the light to our path. Now, however, the Law is no longer our guide; 'if you are led by the Spirit, you are not subject to the law'. It is the same pair of opposites that we have had earlier in the letter (e.g. 3:2).

Paul knew what it was to be led by the Spirit. It involved a complete turn-about in his life and endless travel, not always pleasant because of the conditions both on land and at sea (2 Corinthians 11:23-29). But wherever he went, he carried with him a personality that was no light burden. He describes himself, in another letter, as a 'wretched man', in need of rescue 'from his body of death' (Romans 7:24); and in another as having 'a thorn... in the flesh, a messenger of Satan to torment me' (2 Corinthians 12:7).

The warfare between flesh and Spirit was unceasing inside Paul. He had to choose to walk by the Spirit, guided, enlightened, aided and helped. Paul was not pretending that life would be easier if they were led by the Spirit than if they were under the Law. It would be more difficult. It was a narrow road, hard to travel along.

PRAYER

Help us to endure self-despair.
Help us to resist self.
Help us to follow the Spirit.

30
On the road to destruction

There are two roads: one leads to life and the other to destruction. Paul is exhorting the Galatians to follow the one and avoid the other. He thinks there is no problem in distinguishing them; certainly the results of self-indulgence are obvious. Nevertheless, he gives them a list, to make quite sure that they have got the point.

Though the list begins with 'fornication' and includes 'drunkenness' and 'carousing' it is not limited to sensuality. There are 'religious' sins and social sins also, and in fact there is more concerning the problems of living close to other people, as members of the same body, than about individual acts of wickedness.

The question is: Are we to think of ourselves as moving towards our fulfilment in isolation from other people; even in competition with them? Or are we to think of ourselves as members of an association of people, with obligations to them? In later letters, Paul will use the language of *body* and *organs and limbs*. He did not believe that Christianity was to do with what we do with our solitude.

He was not a individualist. He believed that we were baptized into membership of a group, that Christ was the head of a new humanity, a second Adam; and that the sins we commit against the members of the fellowship are incompatible with its purpose: 'enmities, strife, jealousy, anger, quarrels, dissensions, factions, envy'.

In contrast with the list of 'the fruit of the Spirit' in the next paragraph, this list ends with the words: 'and things like these'. It lacks both shape and conclusion. It is an ugly list of ugly things we do—*works* contrasted with *fruit* (i.e. what the Spirit produces in us).

The hard road leads to *the kingdom of God*; the other, to destruction. 'The kingdom of God' (an expression Paul uses infrequently in his letters: it comes more often in the first three Gospels) means the time when God will reign—after the Lord has come from heaven and abolished all other rulers, human and angelic (1 Corinthians 15:24–28). Paul does not say, 'Sin is of no importance; we shall be saved by faith, therefore it does not matter what we do.' He believes in a future judgment: 'we will all stand before the judgment seat of God' (Romans 14:10). He believes that our present relationship with God (our *justification*) depends on Christ and is known by faith; but our situation on the last day will be according to our deeds (Romans 2:6).

PRAYER

Make us understand that we belong with others.
Let us not sin against them.
Show us how much we need them.

31 On the way to salvation

'The works of the flesh' came in a list that had no unity or overriding shape. It even had no ending: you could add further actions for yourself, if you wished. Evil is destructive and has no cohesion in itself. But what *the Spirit* produces is very different from that: Paul uses a single word to refer to it: *the fruit*. It has unity and shape: the list consists of three threes, and there is no *etcetera* at the end.

Love (Greek *agape*) had to come first, after 5:14: it is the one commandment of God, and all the other aspects of the fruit are further descriptions of love and consequences of it. Notice that *joy* comes second: none of the hardships of the Christian life, to which he referred briefly in verses 16 and 17, in any way take away from joy. He will say elsewhere that the believer is 'always rejoicing' (2 Corinthians 6:10). *Peace* means both peace with God, and (as much as it is possible) with everybody.

The second group of three consists of longer words in Greek, dividing the nine elements into three plus three plus three. *Patience* is willingness to endure irritation; *kindness* is willingness to seek the good of others; and *goodness* is having aims and plans for others; and seeking their welfare.

The third section returns to shorter words: *faithfulness* here is in Greek the word 'faith' that we have heard all through the letter. But perhaps it refers more at this point to faith between believers, rather than between believer and God. *Gentleness* is willingness to be put upon by others; elsewhere it is sometimes translated 'meekness'. It is not a popular characteristic today; it is the opposite of 'thrusting', 'go-getting', etc. *Self-control* is necessary because 'the desires of the flesh' are still at work in the believer.

The nine items on the list are exactly those that one would look for if one were choosing people to be involved in any corporate exercise. They are the essentials for living together and working together; they are what is needed if an association is to be built up and not broken down.

'No law' deals with these matters; they cannot be included in commandments, except for the first, love. They are the opposite of the destructiveness of the flesh (self-centredness). They are the result of God's Spirit, who brings unity out of people who would otherwise be divisive, and creates fellowship among those who might seek their own advantage.

We all agree that the Spirit is the life of the church. Therefore we must be in line with the Spirit, seeking unity with others, allowing the Spirit to produce his fruit in us. The opposite would be conceit, competition, envy.

There is no doubt that Paul understood the meaning of fellowship, community, living together, being part of a society. He stresses it here, at the end of his letter. The trouble-makers have divided the churches: he must heal the divisions that they have made—or rather, the Spirit must re-create the fellowship of the Holy Spirit.

PRAYER

Create the ninefold fruit in us.
Destroy our selfishness.
Bring us into unity.

32
Love in the church

Here, as in his other letters, Paul turns finally to practical matters. How is the love which is the one commandment to be worked out in practice?

First of all, there are still faults within the community: the NRSV translation 'transgression' is unfortunate, since this might be taken to imply that Paul believed in the Law. He uses a different word here from that in 3:19 and it means, literally, 'false step'. He had referred, at the end of the previous paragraph, to conceit, competition and envy. The community is not yet perfect.

The rest of the congregation (if that is what he means by 'you'), filled with God's Spirit, are to restore the one who has erred 'in a spirit of gentleness' (the same word as in 5:23). Such action will tempt them to feelings of superiority and conceit and competition: they are to take care that they resist such temptations. They are to remember that they, too, may fall. One way to do this, is to enter into the problems of others and feel the tensions they are subjected to. This is 'to bear one another's burdens', and this is the law that Christ both taught (e.g. Mark 12:31) and fulfilled by dying for us.

To think oneself something is to assume a status and position before God, from which one can look down on others; as the Pharisee does in the parable (Luke 18:9–14). But this is to forget that our standing before God is entirely through faith in God and Christ. In ourselves, we are nothing. It is remarkably easy for us to deceive ourselves, and take what God has done for us and make it into a reason for looking down on others.

What we have is the fruit of the Spirit (5:22); our own work is the work of God within us. If we recognize that, we shall see how far short it falls of the perfection that it might be. Self-knowledge is the best defence against arrogance and conceit. The load that each of us has to carry is awareness of resistance to the Spirit and failure to be guided by the Spirit.

The apparent contradiction between the command, 'Bear one another's burdens' (v. 2) and, 'All must carry their own loads' (v. 5) calls for some explanation. It is those who know their own problems who will be best at understanding the problems of others; while the reverse is also the case: it is those who are most unaware of their own problems who will be least sympathetic with others.

Paul may have expected the arrival of his letter in Galatia to have promoted reconciliation in the congregations to which it was to be read: some people accusing others of disloyalty to Paul or of lack of insight and faith. He wants to heal the divisions and restore peace to the communities. His letter has been very outspoken, and the situation will now need careful and loving attention.

PRAYER

Help me to put others before myself.
Give me knowledge of myself.
Remind me that I am 'nothing'.

33 You cannot fool God

So far in the letter there has been no reference at all to the ministry in the churches to which Paul is writing; he has addressed the congregations; not their leaders. But now, in 6:6, we have the one and only mention in Galatians of any kind of minister—a 'teacher'. One of the few references to the words of the Lord in Paul's extant letters is in 1 Corinthians 9:14: 'the Lord commanded that those who proclaim the gospel should get their living by the gospel'. This is the purpose of 6:6, extended from the preacher to the teacher: the pupil must share his goods with the teacher—i.e. must pay him for the work he has done.

This unexpected instruction, suddenly coming out of the blue, is then followed by an exhortation to honest thinking and generous doing. One of the ways in which we deceive ourselves is by thinking that God does not know everything, and take everything into account. We think we can fool him. (The word means to turn up your nose at somebody.) This is not how it is with God, and we shall see that it is not when the last day comes and we stand before his judgment seat. On that day (the harvest, the end of the world) we shall 'reap' what we have sown. If, for example, we have spent an unnecessary amount of money on ourselves ('to your own flesh') we shall reap 'corruption' (i.e. God's condemnation): if we have been led by the Spirit into using money for the sake of other people (such as the teacher, mentioned in verse 6) God will reward us with 'eternal life' in the age to come.

This leads Paul to a general conclusion: he exhorts his Galatians to good works, for all and specially for those who belong to the church.

The major part of the letter, 1:1 to 6:10, has been dictated to a scribe; the rest of it, 6:11–18, Paul will write with his own hand. Notice that the last instruction that he gives them in the dictated part of the letter is to work: 'let us work for the good of all...'. Far too often faith has been contrasted with works; as though the believer, the person of faith, was a 'non-doer'; and this way of thinking has been attributed to Paul. In fact, Paul exhorts his hearers to do things and he believes in a God who rewards works that have been performed in love.

Paul's contrast was between the works commanded by the Law (e.g. circumcision, dietary laws, the festivals and sabbaths) and works of love and faith. His final command is to work, while there is still time, and before the Lord comes and time is ended. There is nothing un-Pauline about activity; he was an example of what he taught.

PRAYER

Let us not deceive ourselves.
We cannot fool you.
Make us doers of the word.

34 New creation

Paul's handwriting, which began at this point in the original letter, is larger than that of his scribe. He takes over, to compose a summary of the whole argument and to authenticate the letter. (Compare the end of 2 Thessalonians (3:17): 'I, Paul, write this greeting with my own hand. This is the mark in every letter of mine; it is the way I write.' For the name of one of his scribes, see Romans 16:22.)

The motives of the trouble-makers, he says, are purely selfish: they want the approval of others and they want to avoid persecution. Like Paul (5:11), they would be persecuted if they preached the cross of Christ, for such preaching implies the end of the Law and the unbelief of those who keep it.

Then he says that 'even the circumcised do not themselves obey the law', possibly meaning that his opponents in Galatia are not themselves as perfect in their observances as they should be—or as he had been in the past, when he was 'far more zealous' than many of his contemporaries 'for the traditions of his ancestors' (1:14). He was an expert; they are mere amateurs. And their motivation is this: they can boast about the number of converts they have made, converts to a system that he denigrates as 'flesh'.

Paul's life, as he showed us at the beginning of the letter, fell into two parts: before his conversion and after. The turning point was God's revelation of his Son; the one who had been crucified was the Lord. For Paul to change was like death and resurrection: the world was crucified to him, and he to the world (compare 2:19). All his ideas about God and how to live have been changed. He can no longer boast about converts and numbers as (he says) his opponents are doing. He can only boast about the cross. What before looked like shame is now seen to be God's glory. Weakness is strength, foolishness is wisdom. It is a 'new creation' that he is living in. He prays for peace and mercy upon those who see what he says and live by it: they are God's Israel, the true people of God. (This seems to be the meaning here, but it is much disputed; see REB footnote.)

Paul lived through a revolution and came out the other side a changed man. His priorities were altered and everything was turned upside down. His letter to the Galatians is an attempt to share his understanding with others, and if he is at times very outspoken and extremely blunt it's understandable.

To have read his letter is to have been invited to think his thoughts after him and to share his new insights. He has invited everyone who hears what he is saying, to live the life of a new creation in what remains of the old.

PRAYER

'I have been crucified with Christ'
May I never forget that!
Make me live to you.

35
The guarantee of genuineness

Paul's final sentences sum up much of the argument of the letter as a whole and leave the readers (or hearers) of it where he wants them to be—not where they were going before he began to write and they to hear what he had written.

There is no doubt that he has been troubled by the situation: it has aroused his anger and driven him to speak his mind. 'From now on' he hopes no one need raise these questions (of the observances of the Law by Gentile believers) again. He has given them the answer. But if they do still question him he has the final irrefutable reply for all to see, in the marks made in his flesh. He had been beaten with the thirty-nine lashes, five times; this was the punishment administered in synagogues. He had also been the victim of a stoning (2 Corinthians 11:24-25). You could see it, if you looked at him; and that was the proof that he no longer preached the Law. He was now the servant of Jesus—and he preached the cross, and was persecuted for it. His scars were his guarantee.

He will tell the Corinthians, later, about people who came to Corinth with letters of recommendation (2 Corinthians 3:1): written evidence from someone else that they were genuine. He carries his recommendation on his back and in his skin: he has been punished in the synagogues. He has changed from Law-keeper to gospel-preacher and the evidence is his rejection by those who used to be his associates.

He had said that there was a new creation (6:15); in it, everything is upside down. Rejection is acceptance, failure to persuade is proof of success; humiliation is honour.

This is how it had been with Jesus, and the slave of Jesus is marked with the same signs. Paul will develop this line of argument in a later letter to Corinth (2 Corinthians). Here, he leaves the whole matter like a time-bomb waiting to go off. Everyone reading 6:17 can work it out for themselves.

In conclusion he prays for them to live in 'the grace of our Lord

Jesus Christ'—his favour, which is also God's favour. This is to fill their 'spirits'—and they need no longer worry about the flesh. They are his 'brothers and sisters', even though they have been foolish, bewitched, unsettled and on the edge of falling away from Christ. He is confident that his letter will keep them in God's love.

PRAYER

Thank you for Paul, his clarity and persuasiveness.
Thank you for Christ, his love and his grace.
Thank you for your knowledge of us.

NOTES

NOTES

NOTES

NOTES

NOTES

NOTES

NOTES

NOTES

NOTES

NOTES

PBC
voucher
GAL
01

THE PEOPLE'S
BIBLE COMMENTARY
VOUCHER SCHEME

The People's Bible Commentary (PBC) provides a range of readable, accessible commentaries. These will grow into a library that will eventually cover the whole Bible.

A voucher is printed on the last page of each People's Bible Commentary Volume (as above). These vouchers count towards free copies of other volumes in the series.

• 4 purchases of PBC volumes entitle the reader to a further volume (up to the value of £7.99) FREE

• 6 purchases of PBC volumes entitle the reader to a further volume (up to the value of £9.99) FREE

You should find a coupon for the PBC voucher scheme inserted loose with this volume. If for some reason the coupon is missing, please ask at your local bookshop or contact BRF direct to obtain a replacement.

All you need do:

• Cut out the appropriate vouchers from the last page of the PBCs you have purchased and attach them to the coupon.

• Complete your name and address details, and indicate your choice of free entitlement from the list on the coupon.

• Take the coupon to your local Christian Bookshop who will exchange it for your free PBC volume; or send the coupon direct to BRF who will send you your free PBC volume. Please allow 28 days for delivery.

Please note that PBC volumes provided under the voucher scheme are subject to availability. If your first choice is not available, you may be sent your second choice volume.

BRF, Peter's Way, Sandy Lane West, Oxford OX4 5HG
Tel 01865 748227   Fax 01865 773150 Registered Charity No. 233280